KATIE HOFF

Blueprint

An Olympian's Story of Striving, Adapting, and Embracing the Suck

Author: Katie Hoff
Coauthor: Richard Bader
Contributing Editor: Marla McKenna
Associate Editor: Griffin Mill
Proofreader: Lyda Rose Haerle
Interior Layout: Michael Nicloy
Cover Design: Maury Page, Mevo Creative Studios

Cover and Author Photos: Maury Page
Hair and Make up by Abby Schnoover, Brown & DeLine

All photos courtesy of Katie Hoff unless otherwise noted

Published by: CG Sports Publishing
Head of Publishing: Michael Nicloy

Katie Hoff Representation: Cejih Yung, CG Sports Management
www.cgsportsmanagement.com

Hold your phone's camera up to this
code to watch welcome video!

IPHONE   ANDROID

ISBN: 978-1-7359193-0-0

Produced and Distributed by NXI Press,
a division of Nico 11 Publishing & Design

Quantity order requests can be emailed to:
mike@nico11publishing.com

Printed in The United States of America

To my parents, John and Jeanne.

My foundation. I would never be as resilient, strong, or able to keep getting back up without your love, support, and understanding.

To my husband, Todd.

The love of my life. You hold me together with your patience, love, and unwavering support. I could never have had the strength to write this memoir without you.

BLUEPRINT

An Olympian's Story of Striving, Adapting,
and Embracing the Suck

BY

KATIE HOFF

WITH RICHARD BADER

AUTHOR'S NOTE

Dear Reader,

There are some swimming terms in this book that may be unfamiliar to some of you. Please see the terms I use most below. Please note also that any race length I talk about is in *meters*, unless otherwise noted in *yards*.

IM - *Individual Medley (all 4 strokes, butterfly, backstroke, breaststroke, freestyle)*

Olympics and Olympic Trials format - *50 meter pool*

Grand Prix format (in my case) - *50 meter pool*

Short Course - *25 meter or 25 yard pool*

Long Course - *50 meter pool*

BLUEPRINT

"…the most important thing in life is not the triumph, but the struggle."

- Pierre de Coubertin, father of the modern Olympics

Embrace the suck: (military, slang)

To accept something that is extremely unpleasant but unavoidable.
The situation is bad, but deal with it.

"I'm off the deep end. Watch as I dive in."

- Lady Gaga, from the song, "Shallow"

PROLOGUE

B^{link.}

Go on. Blink your eyes.

How long do you think that took? A fraction of a second, for sure, but what fraction? A quarter of a second? A fifth? A "split" second, whatever that means?

Google it. Google it and you'll find that for the average person, a blink takes about a tenth of a second. Pretty fast, in other words.

Now let's put that tenth of a second in context. Say you're in the Olympics, a swimmer, and you're racing for a gold medal. The race is 400 meters long, eight lengths of a 50-meter pool, and you're swimming freestyle. At the last turn, with one length of the pool to go, you're ahead, by about a full body length, which at the Olympics is a lot. Thirty meters from the finish and you're still winning, but the swimmer in second place has started to close the gap. Ten meters out, your lead continues to shrink, but it still looks like you're heading for gold. Five meters.

Four. Three. Two. You stretch. You reach out for the wall. But you're not the only one reaching for the wall. The swimmer two lanes over, the British girl, the one who has been closing that gap, is reaching for it, too. Blink now, and you'll miss the most important part.

That race, of course, is not hypothetical. It's my race. The year is 2008, and the pool is at what they called the Water Cube, the blue bubble-sided swimming venue for the 2008 Olympic Games in Beijing. Everyone who follows swimming even a little bit remembers that Olympics because it's the one where Michael Phelps won eight gold medals, breaking a record that had stood for 36 years. Some in the media called me "the female Phelps," because I was supposed to come home from Beijing with a bunch of gold hanging around my neck, too. I didn't discourage the label. Mine may not have been a household name like his, and I wasn't going to win eight gold medals, but winning four wasn't out of the question. Or now three, as the day before this race I finished third in the 400-individual medley, an event I was favored to win. The swimmer who won that race broke the world record I had held. Third place means bronze, and bronze is nice, but it's not gold.

The 400-freestyle is not my best event, and in this one I'm not the favorite. And yet when I do my flip turn and push off the wall for the last time and head into the final 50 meters, I'm ahead by enough that it looks like I've got this one.

At the finish, if you watch a video of the race, you can't tell who gets there first. But the wall—the high-tech wall with its state-of-the-art micro-sensors—the wall knows. And it's not me. I touch second, by seven hundredths of a second, or less time than it takes to blink.

Finishing second at the Olympics means you win a silver medal, and for most people, winning a silver medal at the Olympics would rank high among the greatest achievements of their lives. But if people are calling you "the female Phelps," in the eyes of the world, all finishing second means is you lost.

I've only watched that video once, and that was by accident. Why don't I watch it? Because I don't have to. I know what happened.

I live with what happened every day of my life. It's changed my life, but for worse? For better? At the time I was sure it was for the worse. But now, I'm not so sure.

You can dive off into your life with the most precise blueprint for how it should unfold, but things don't always go the way you planned. At least for me they didn't.

This is my story.

PART 1

ON YOUR MARK...

I didn't start out as a swimmer, or at least I didn't start out as a very good one. I was five years old, and my parents had just moved from California—from Sunnyvale, in the Bay Area, south of Palo Alto—to Williamsburg, Virginia. We lived in an area called Kingspoint, just north of the James River, because that's where my grandparents lived.

My thing at that time was dance—tap, ballet, jazz, whatever they'd let a five-year-old do. But in the summer in Williamsburg, the older kids in my neighborhood would swim on a team at a local pool. Like any five-year-old who aspires to be a seven-year-old, I told my parents I wanted to swim too. To my five-year-old eyes, swimming on the team looked to be what the cool kids did, and I wanted to be cool like them. And the ribbons they awarded for swimming came in pretty colors. Pink and purple were my favorite colors, so those were the ribbons I wanted most. So what if you got them for finishing in sixth and seventh place.

Being a cool kid was one thing. Being a cold kid was another, and on that swimming team, I was cold a lot. I was a skinny five-year-old with zero body fat, and I would shake and shiver in and out of the pool. I hated being cold, and I wasn't all that crazy about the practices or the meets, either. "I want to stop," I told my mom. So at age six, I retired from swimming.

I kept dancing. My number one skill was that I could do all three of the splits—to the right, to the left, and in the middle—and as a reward for my splits skills I got my name posted on the dance bulletin board. This was a big deal, a tangible record of my accomplishment, posted there for all the world to see, or at least for the world that encompassed my dance classes to see. I liked that dance bulletin board. Then and now, I like places where you get to update your progress and see a record of what you've done. Many years later, when I would work in the corporate world, I would obsess over the board where we recorded sales, so much that people I worked with would wonder what was wrong with me. That obsession started in my dance classes.

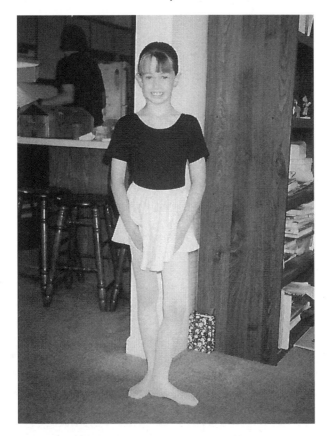

My desire to be the best at splits foreshadowed other traits that would emerge. I was an intense little girl—intense and competitive. When I'd be in a car with my parents and we'd drive through a tunnel, I'd want to hold my breath longer than my little brother could (this would turn out to be an important crossover skill when I returned to swimming). When we'd get back to our house, I'd race to beat him up the steps to our door. This was not terribly difficult when we were little, because when I was six, my brother Christian was two. It got more challenging as we got older.

I liked to win, plain and simple, and with dance, I couldn't figure out a way to win. So, when I was seven, I told my parents I wanted to give swimming another try.

"Something went off in her head," my mom said, "and she decided she didn't want to be beaten anymore."

My earlier attempts at racing.

My mom, Jeanne, holding my one-week-old brother, Christian; and me.

Returning to the Kingspoint Dolphins was frustrating. Anna Linkenauger was winning. The Murphy sisters were winning. I wasn't winning, and I wanted to know why they were, and I wasn't. One big reason was that they weren't just swimming in the summer, like I was, but they were swimming year-round, with the Williamsburg Aquatic Club. So, I joined the Williamsburg Aquatic Club.

Me and my good friend Allison Wilhelm.
She made my first experience on swim team so fun!

We practiced at an indoor pool, and that helped with feeling cold all the time. We were supposed to practice twice a week, on Tuesday and Sunday evenings, even though more than once I'd be sitting with my family at dinner on a Sunday evening and my mom and I would look at each other and realize we'd forgotten about practice. I still had some learning to do about dedication.

I would even sometimes cheat a little bit in practice. If we were supposed to do walking lunges around the pool deck, I would watch for the coach's head to turn and then just walk normally for a few steps to give myself a break. Sometimes for long pool swims—in the 50-meter pool—I'd stop in the middle of a lap and turn around and head back the other way, disguising the move in a way that (I hoped) the coaches wouldn't notice.

But I'd come to love swimming, and with time those bad habits went away. I had an old swimsuit that, if I won the fight with my mom, I'd get to wear to bed a couple days a week. When I got to practice, I would run from our family's minivan into the rec center wearing nothing but that swimsuit, my swim cap, and goggles.

By the time I was nine, I had turned into sort of a monster. What kind of monster? The kind who didn't just want to win when I swam but *had* to win. The kind who would write down every time for everything I swam, down to the hundredth of a second, and I would update it meticulously after every practice or meet. The kind who would walk up to other kids at meets and ask them their times, just so I could tell them my times, which were faster. I mean, how annoying is that?

I hated losing anywhere, at anything. Both of my parents are competitive. My mom was a great athlete, an outstanding basketball player for Stanford, who set scoring records in the early 1980s. She's in the Stanford Athletic Hall of Fame. My dad combines his competitiveness with a bit of an obsessive streak. He and my mom met at Stanford, and in the first year of their marriage he was convinced that he could beat her at basketball. So

Me, my brother Christian, and our dad.

they'd play one-on-one, and she would win again and again. But he kept trying. They even got into a fight about it. I'm grateful that I inherited both of those traits. That combination—a competitive spirit with obsessive tendencies—can be really positive for an athlete, giving you both the motivation to do something and the discipline you need to achieve it. It's a powerful blend, unless it crosses a line. Sometimes I crossed that line.

I remember being in school in fourth grade—that was the one year I wasn't homeschooled—and in Phys Ed we were doing pullups. This other kid, a boy, did 14, and I did 12. He beat me, and it made me furious. To this day, more than 20 years later, I can still remember his name, but I won't say it because he's in his early 30s now, and it would just sound silly.

Pull ups were such a proud source of strength for me throughout my career.

I could get hyper-competitive in miniature golf, or bowling, or board games. I once threw a fit at a sleepover, furious at how a dance competition we'd thought up for ourselves—involving songs by the Backstreet Boys and Shania Twain—was stacked unfairly against my teammate and me. I could be a little too intense. This didn't endear me to friends or sometimes even to my own family. When I was 11, we went on a vacation to a cabin in West Virginia, and we set up a badminton court. My grandmother and I were on the same team, and I got frustrated because I thought she wasn't playing well enough. Eventually we had to end the game because I started verbally assaulting my own grandma. That was it—no more family games for the rest of that trip.

✳✳✳

In the pool, it would nag me to my core if I didn't swim the times I knew I could swim, or if I didn't beat swimmers who I normally beat in practice. As much as I hated losing pullup battles in gym class, I really hated losing in the water. I'd be all consumed by this. Some swimmers can just go out and crush it in a meet, regardless of what they've done in practice, but I was never like that. I had to prove what I could do in practice, to give myself confidence for what I could do in a meet.

Around this time, I had an epiphany. At practice we were doing fast 50-yard repeats, and on one of the repeats I realized that I could dig deeper. I could kick harder. I could pull harder. It was like I'd found another gear. It hurt more, sure, but I discovered that if I worked hard enough and accepted the discomfort that would come from working harder, I had this new untapped reservoir that I could draw from. I told my mom and dad after that practice that I had discovered "deep down" speed. And when I shifted into deep down speed, I could beat kids who were two, three, sometimes four years older than me. It was an amazing feeling.

There's this term that comes from the military called "embracing the suck." It basically means that you're going to accept that something is going to be really uncomfortable, but you're going to do it anyway. I've never been in the military, but I'm picturing 5:00 a.m. obstacle courses in full combat gear, things like that—things that push you and make you a better soldier. That's basically what I was doing in the pool. Deep down speed wasn't easy, and it wasn't fun, but it was incredibly satisfying.

★★★

At nine I made my first Zone team. USA Swimming, the governing body for the sport in the U.S., divided the country into four Zones—Eastern, Western, Southern, and Central—and Virginia, where I swam, was in the Eastern Zone. Each Zone holds different regional meets every year, and to make a Zone team, you have to be in the top two in the state in your age group. My times were fast enough that I qualified.

We got on a bus, and as I recall we went to Buffalo. I was on Team Virginia, and at nine I was competing against some girls who were 10 and about to turn 11. Some of them were starting to go through puberty, and I was far, far from that. I was still this really tiny, really skinny kid. My mom would force-feed me with Ensure and Boost, drinks that adults drink to keep their weight up. Also, Dairy Queen milkshakes. And Snickers bars. And Arby's curly fries. Making Zones was a big deal to me. At Zones they would give you stuff—swimsuits, warmups, things like that—and that was motivating—it made me feel like a real athlete. I felt proud to qualify, but it still wasn't like I was some phenom swimmer. My first time in Zones, I swam the 200-individual medley, and I think I finished in 11th place.

In the summer after Zones I broke my first Virginia state record at the State Championships in Newport News, in the 100-breaststroke. I remember there was a picture of me in the local newspaper, and my mouth was wide open because I couldn't believe that I'd broken the record. I was the fastest swimmer in the state in the 9-10 age group in the 100-breaststroke. It was at that point that I started thinking, *okay, I want to do this. I want to be the best at this.*

The path to becoming the best had some potholes. When I got disqualified in a backstroke race for doing an illegal flip turn, I was furious, embarrassed, and mortified. It was as if the world had done me an injustice. I went home in tears.

"What's wrong?" my dad asked.

I mumbled something about needing to be better than a swimmer who got herself disqualified for doing a bad flip turn.

And I announced that I was going to swim in the Olympics.

I was 10 years old.

FORMATIVE YEARS

My coach at Williamsburg Aquatic Club was Harold Baker, and even though I was only with him for about a year or a year and a half, I think he was just about the perfect first coach for me. Even as a little kid I was super nervous at meets, super high-strung. I'd go off to wait behind the starting blocks way before it was time to line up for a heat. I'd press my goggles into my eye sockets over and over, many more times than I needed to make sure they wouldn't leak. (The goggles thing was a quirk that stayed throughout my swimming career.) Harold was the club's head coach, overseeing everybody at every age, but he would find time to come up to me before a race and say something just to calm me down. He'd tell me to just go have fun, just go enjoy it. That was probably the perfect thing for a coach to say to me at that point in my life. He was a great first coach.

My other coach in Williamsburg was Rich Williams. Rich was young, in his early 20s, and he had this energy. He could pump me full of confidence. I remember once we were at a practice at the pool at the College of William & Mary in Williamsburg. I would get super red in the face when I swam—it had something to do with not processing my sweating very well—and he got me out in front of all of the other kids, pointed to my red face, and said, "This is what your face should look like when you swim!" as if my rosy complexion was all about effort and not just about a quirk of physiology. The other kids must have hated me. Rich had an intensity that I really thrived off of.

My first coach Harold Baker and me at JO's (state champs).

In 2000, Rich left Williamsburg Aquatic Club to work at Poseidon Swimming, about an hour away in Richmond. I had just turned 11, and I followed him there, which meant my parents had to drive back and forth to Richmond multiple times a week to get me to and from practices.

Turning 11 meant moving up into the 11-12 age group. It's an odd age group, and what makes it odd is puberty. Some girls at that age are still little girls, while others are starting to develop into young women. I was still a little girl, and a super nervous little girl at that. I didn't feel confident. I was losing, a lot, and I even thought about quitting because I was losing so much. I'd done well in the 9-10s, winning multiple times at Zone meets and breaking some state records, but competing with the 11-12s was a whole different kettle of fish.

At a Zone meet when I was 11, my nervous energy wa. getting the better of me. I felt defeat in my mind, and doubt in the pit of my stomach. I liked to wake up early at meets, to help me feel ready. On the morning of the first day of Zones, I got up before my alarm clock went off, put on my fancy Speedo Aquablade racing suit, threw on some warmups and headed down to the hotel restaurant for breakfast. The hallways seemed dimmer than they should have been. And emptier—no one was out moving about. When I got to the hotel lobby, I saw a clock on the wall. It was 3:30 in the morning. My alarm clock in my room wouldn't go off for another three and a half hours. I went back up to my room, ate a nutrition bar, and lay in bed at war with my nerves, trying, and mostly failing, to fall asleep until it was time to get up.

Rich Williams with Mollie Wilson (a teammate of mine)
and me at one of my first Zone trips.

Longer races made me more nervous than shorter ones. In shorter races, I would just go all out. In longer races, there's strategy, there's the pain, there's the duration of the race, there's the possibility of dying at the end (not really, but it sometimes felt like that). It just seemed like there was more that could go wrong in a longer race. At Zones, I was scheduled to swim two longer races: the 400-yard individual medley and the 500-yard freestyle. At age 11, I just didn't feel ready for that kind of race.

prelims for the 500-yard free, I was a nervous
my best to fake smiles with my teammates and
coach's advice. Ten minutes before the race, as I
headed toward the blocks, I didn't feel well at all. A savvy
parent chaperone picked up on my discomfort and asked if
she could help. And then all of my fear, stress, and anxiety just
gushed out of me, along with my breakfast. I threw up all over
the pool deck and all over this nice lady's shoes. The race didn't
go too well, either.

✶✶✶

During this whole time—except for a little while in
kindergarten and that brief period during fourth grade—my
mom homeschooled me. My dad worked in sales, and my mom
stayed home with me and my brother. Homeschooling fit great
with my swimming schedule. I saw so many kids coming to
practice looking exhausted from the school day or staying up
late to study for tests. I remember seeing that and thinking how
lucky I was. I went back to a "real" school briefly in fourth grade
because I asked if I could go, but after I went back, I failed to see
what was so great about it, and we went back to homeschooling.
I was a good student but what I was really invested in was
swimming. It was all about priorities.

VA teammates at one of my first Zone trips.

Rich and me at JO's on Poseidon.

Homeschooling however, didn't work out to be the best thing for my relationship with my mom. As I got older, we would get in screaming matches, fighting over assignments or grades. We kept battling until I finished middle school, at which point she became worried that homeschooling was hurting our relationship too much. Besides, she reasoned, we would need official transcripts for me to get into college. So then I enrolled in what's called The American School, which is a homeschool program that sends you all the course materials and takes care of things like transcripts and diplomas, items you need to apply to college. It turned out to be a good compromise for both academic and domestic reasons.

Meanwhile, working with Rich Williams at Poseidon Swimming in Richmond really made a mark on me as a young energy before a race was infectious. It wasn't like 'Hey, you're going to be in the Olympics someday," me a lot of confidence. It turned out I made an impres̲ ̲ on him as a coach, too. Years later he would tell me that it wasn't until meeting me that he realized how far an athlete could push herself.

After I swam for about a year with Poseidon, Rich decided to stop coaching for a while. And, Diane Cayce, another of the Poseidon coaches, left to go to Typhoon Aquatics, in Newport News, Virginia. Newport News is a lot closer to Williamsburg than Richmond is, so I left Poseidon and joined Typhoon Aquatics.

Watch one of my first interviews ever.

Diane Cayce and me, on our way to my first nationals in Fort Lauderdale.

I began training with a group of boys who were several years older than I was. They teased me. They picked on me. I was an easy target, being younger and being prone to reacting which only served to encourage them. Some of this was in fun, but some of it went past fun. They would swim behind me and push my feet sideways to wreck any rhythm or momentum I had in the pool. They would hide my equipment. They would tell adult jokes they knew that I, at age 13, wouldn't get.

My response was to swim harder, hard enough that in 2002 I qualified for the Long Course National Championships in the 200-individual medley. That meant I was going to Fort Lauderdale.

Qualifying for the 2002 National Championships felt like an out-of-body experience. You qualify for Nationals by the times you swim, so qualifying meant I was swimming national-caliber times, which was a thrill but also very strange.

All of my heroes were in Fort Lauderdale—Jenny Thompson, Natalie Coughlin, Maggie Bowen—swimmers I had idolized for years. I had Jenny Thompson's poster on my bedroom wall. These swimmers were icons. So what was I doing there?

At the risk of repeating some insights into the psychology of me, I'm someone who has to be confident in my training and in what I've been able to do in the past, in the pool, in order to perform my best at meets. If I've swum well in practice consistently, then I'm confident that I'll swim well at a meet. The reverse of that is also true. If I haven't had the opportunity to prepare, or if my preparation hasn't gone as well as I wanted it to, then I feel unsure of myself coming into a meet. That lack of confidence can translate into a sub par performance.

Unfortunately for me as a competitor, to a certain degree the same thing applies when I'm in new environments. Familiar environments don't faze me. Unfamiliar environments do, or at least have the potential to. The U.S. National Swimming Championships in Fort Lauderdale was definitely one of those unfamiliar environments. There were Olympians in Fort Lauderdale. These swimmers were among the best of the best. I had never swum against them before. I struggled to convince myself I belonged.

There's only so much a coach can do in a situation like this. The Typhoon Aquatics coaches were supportive. But their advice? "Stay calm, relax, have fun." That advice may have been fine when I was nine. It was less helpful when I was 13, and in the years that followed. *Relax? Have fun? How am I supposed to have fun? I'm freaking out!*

Fort Lauderdale was a learning experience for everyone. My coaches had a nervous, high-strung, and somewhat intimidated 13-year old on their hands who didn't respond really well to, "Don't worry—everything will be fine." I swam in just one event in Fort Lauderdale—the 200-individual medley. Everything was not fine. I finished in 37th place.

Later in the meet, I was standing on the pool deck when Natalie Coughlin set a world record in the 100-backstroke, becoming the first woman ever to swim that event in under a minute. Some people see something like that and they're starstruck by it. They put the person who accomplished it up on a pedestal. I was happy for Natalie, but what I felt in that moment wasn't awe. The distance between us had narrowed. For me, strangely, seeing her set that world record left me feeling both inspired and challenged. Challenged in the sense that even though she was seven years older than me and had already won gold medals in international competitions, if she could do that, why couldn't I do that, too? And that was inspiring. It helped crystallize what I was aiming for.

One of my first Grand Prix meets in Charlotte.
I still slammed my goggles into my face nonstop during this time period.

My goals shifted. The bar got raised. When I was 10, I wanted to be an Olympic swimmer. After I saw Natalie set that world record, being an Olympic swimmer was no longer enough. I wanted to be a world-record holder. I wanted to be a gold medalist, because look what she just did.

NBAC

Earlier in 2002, I had been at a sectional meet where I met Courtney Kalisz, who lived in Maryland and swam for North Baltimore Aquatic Club. NBAC had built quite a reputation for developing quality swimmers and had been sending swimmers to the Olympics for nearly 20 years—people like Theresa Andrews, Anita Nall, and Beth Botsford. In 2002, one of those Olympians was a teenager by the name of Michael Phelps. At age 15 he'd finished 5th in the 200-butterfly at the Sydney Olympics in 2000, and people were beginning to expect more great things from him. We all know how that worked out. Thanks to NBAC, Baltimore had become something of a mecca for swimmers. NBAC had an aura of greatness. As a kid, you walk onto the pool deck at NBAC's home pool at the Meadowbrook Aquatic Center and it's like, *you want to swim here? Remember, Olympians swim here.*

Courtney and I became friends, and after years of mostly training with guys who were older than me, I thought it could be good to have a female training partner who was around my age. I went to Baltimore and had a trial practice with Paul Yetter, who was one of the NBAC coaches. The practice went well, and

I had a good rapport with Paul. He would tell me what times he wanted me to swim for what intervals and how many times I needed to swim them. That made so much more sense to me than just being told to "swim hard" or "go faster." Paul was as obsessive about times as I was. I liked his precision. I liked his intensity. I felt comfortable with him immediately. I thought he could be the perfect coach for me.

The Long Course National Championships in 2003 were in College Park, Maryland. With my experience a year earlier of swimming at the Nationals in Fort Lauderdale under my belt, I went into it feeling much better prepared, and I came out of it with much better results. I finished fourth in the 200-IM, which was a big improvement on 37th place, though me being me, I still found a way to undercut my own performance. A lot of the swimmers on the U.S. National Team weren't in College Park because they were in Barcelona competing at the 2003 World Championships. That meant the competition at Nationals wasn't as stiff as it would have been otherwise. So I said to myself, *yeah, I finished fourth, but look who <u>wasn't</u> here.* That sounds like I'm throwing cold water on my accomplishments, but I'd like to think that's just me being realistic, not pessimistic. Still, I had swum a solid time in the 200-IM, and I dropped something like six seconds off my best time in the 400-IM.

My dad's work at that time was taking him to Maryland more and more. I was swimming better, and ready to take the next step in my career. NBAC had a coach and a training partner I liked. So at the end of the summer of 2003, we moved to Maryland.

We moved into a townhouse in Abingdon, north and east of Baltimore City and about 40 minutes from NBAC's home pool at Meadowbrook, in Baltimore's Mount Washington neighborhood. I didn't swim at Meadowbrook. We swam at an NBAC satellite location near Abingdon, at a place called Knight Diver, in a pool used for scuba diving lessons. The pool was under a sort of tent-bubble, had just four lanes, and was beyond dinky and dark, and had bad ventilation. I would have coughing fits because the air was so bad at practice. Nothing about it screamed, "Olympian!" It was just this crazy, crappy pool with four lanes and 12 kids in a group.

Shortly after making the move to Maryland, I sat down with Paul. I had already swum times that qualified me for the 2004 Olympic Trials in the 200-IM and the 400-IM. I told him that my goal was to make an Olympic Trials final, which means going to trials and finishing in the top eight. True, this goal was a step or two below what I'd told myself in Fort Lauderdale about wanting to be a world record holder and an Olympic gold medalist. But I figured I was still a few rungs below that level. I didn't even think actually making the Olympic team was realistic at that point. I just thought, *if I can be in the top eight in 2004, that would be amazing.*

Something about a new team, a new coach, and the magic Olympic year ignited my fire to be perfect and obsessive in my process even further. There were so many moments where I demanded perfection of myself to an extreme. And sometimes to near death!

One Saturday morning practice thereafter, we were tasked with doing 10x200 yard repeats. I just couldn't get into that "deep down" gear to hit the paces that Paul had so meticulously planned out for me. I was devastated. My mom picked me up, and we headed home. I couldn't let it go. The fact that I had missed my paces consumed me. I got home, ate breakfast, and couldn't take it. I called Paul and asked if I could come in later that afternoon to do the set over again. I didn't want to leave one stone unturned. Later that afternoon, I went back to the pool with vengeance in my heart and I hit pace every single 200. My confidence soared.

In that same period, my dad was driving me to practice on a Saturday afternoon after a swim meet. The meet did not have the 400-yard IM in that particular session, and Paul and I wanted to test out where my times were. We had set up a "time trial" that afternoon. My dad put his blinker on to take the next exit on the highway. I screamed out, "Dad! This isn't it. We have one more exit. We will be late if we go the wrong way!" My dad calmly reassured me that this was correct. Mind you, this was before a GPS just told you where to go. Panic filled me at the thought of even being one minute late to practice. And at NBAC, 10 minutes early behind the blocks was on time. Nine minutes early was late.

It was time to take matters into my own hands. I turned to my dad in the driver's seat and said calmly but affirmatively, "Dad, if you take this exit, I'm going to rip the steering wheel out of your hands." My dad still recounts the story to this day and says he had to decide quickly if his daughter was really going to do something that crazy. Luckily, within a few seconds of my psychotic statement, I came to my senses and realized my dad was correct. A sense of direction has never been my strong suit. In my defense, I really, really didn't want to be late. People who want to break world records just *were not* late. At least that was my rationale.

As a tune-up for the Olympic Trials, NBAC took a team to California for the Santa Clara Grand Prix. I won the 400-IM, and dropped about three seconds off my best time. At the time, a bunch of us were all hovering around a time of 4:42 in that event. Dropping three seconds, to 4:39, was a huge milestone. It meant I would be ranked first going into the Olympic Trials. For the first time, I really believed I could make an Olympic team. I flew home from Santa Clara feeling elated. I thought, *this could actually happen.*

ATHENS

When I was 10, I idolized the great swimmers. I read *Splash*, the magazine of USA Swimming, religiously. I collected these insert magazines inside *Splash* that had features of top swimmers—Jenny Thompson, or Amy Van Dyken, or Tom Dolan, or Brooke Bennett—all those people who were the stars, all those swimmers I looked up to. When I was 11, I watched the Olympics on television for the first time and saw Kaitlin Sandeno win a medal when she was 17 years old. I thought, *I'm breaking state records now—maybe I can do what she's doing before too long.* It felt within reach. At the time, I didn't know what going to the Olympics meant, or what went into it, or how you qualified for it. For me it was just, I love swimming, and I love winning, and with that kind of blind confidence I felt like I could get there. Blind confidence might be the best kind to have, because to know what actually goes into it could be paralyzing.

The 2004 Olympic Trials were in Long Beach, California, and I qualified in the 200-IM and the 400-IM. I don't want to overstate that accomplishment. You could have the 75th best time in the nation in an event and qualify for the Olympic Trials. Some 700 or more people were there, with eight or nine heats of each event.

31

My mom encouraged me to take up journaling, and I found this years later. Crazy to think that I predicted the future at just 12 years old.

People qualify for trials and get labeled "Olympic hopeful," though I'm thinking, *wait a minute, let's slow down a little*. You make trials, that's one level. Then you have to make it through the preliminary races to the finals, and that puts you at another level. And then to make the Olympic team, you have to finish first or second in the finals. That's a lot different than just qualifying for trials. Making the Olympic trial cut and actually going to the Olympics are two very different things.

In the prelims for the 400-IM, I didn't swim a good race or a smart race. I was super nervous, and I started way too fast, and when you do that you pay for it at the finish. I was in a lot of pain when I got out of the pool, barely able to walk, with lactic acid levels through the roof. I gained almost 10 seconds on my best time, and all I could think about afterward was how badly I'd blown it, how I'd just wrecked my chances of going to the Olympics. Luckily, I still finished sixth, which qualified me for the final. That meant I had reached one goal I set for myself—swimming in an Olympic Trials final.

I tried unsuccessfully to take a nap, then got something to eat, and by the time I was back at the pool for finals I felt like a different person. I had a great warmup, so that helped a lot too.

Associated Press
Wide World Photos

SWIM TRIALS: Katie Hoff, 15, center, smiles after receiving a medal and a flag from Janet Evans, left, after winning the Women's 400 Meter Individual Medley finals with a time of 4:37.67 at the U.S. Olympic swim trials in Long Beach, Calif., Wednesday, July 7, 2004. (AP Photo/Mark J. Terrill) (MJT110 - 20040707)

Still, I was as surprised as anybody when I won the 400-IM with a time that was within shouting distance of the American record. It wasn't a perfect race—I hit my butt on the wall on my backstroke turn—but I smiled for the whole last 50 meters and kept smiling with the cameras on me at the end. I couldn't sleep that night I was so happy. Two days later, I won the 200-IM as well. Not only would I be going to Athens, but I would be going as the top American seed in two events.

The two most important hugs—a hug from my mom and a hug from my dad after winning the 400 IM at Olympic Trials and making my first Olympic team.

Watch my race!

After I made the Olympic swimming team, I didn't go right to the Olympics, nor did I get to go home. I went straight to training camp, the first stop on a long haul of six weeks. From Long Beach, we went to Stanford University for training camp. When I left home to go to trials, I didn't take a lot of things with me, because I would have felt embarrassed to have all of these big suitcases with me and then not make the team and have to fly home with them to Maryland. So when I went with the team to Stanford, my mom had to mail clothes to me.

At Stanford, the training went well, but socially it was a little bit weird. There were a couple of other girls who were close to my age—I remember Dana Vollmer was 16—but even so, at 15, I had the stigma of being the young one. It wasn't like I was this mature 15-year-old. I was naïve. I'd been homeschooled. My first roommate at camp was going around telling people I needed a nightlight. I didn't need a nightlight—I just wanted the door cracked so I could see into the bathroom when it was dark. But when I found out that she was saying that about me, I thought, *c'mon, are we really going to do this?* And that wasn't the only example. I would get kicked out of the lane I was swimming in during the middle of a set. I'd get snapped at for asking questions that I thought made sense, but that the older swimmers made me feel were stupid. It just wasn't very warm and welcoming. Here I was, the youngest swimmer on the team, and maybe the youngest of all the U.S. Olympic athletes. You'd think these women, many of whom were in their mid-20s, would see that maybe this 15-year-old rookie needed some support.

And to be fair, it wasn't like everybody was doing these things to me. I remember Maritza Correia, a 22-year-old freestyler, saw how some of the girls were treating me. She went to Jenny Thompson, the team captain, and to the head coach, and told them what was going on. They immediately addressed the problem, and I was grateful. After that a few people came up to me and said, "Hey, you don't need to put up with this."

I don't blame anybody for the way things went. When you're in that environment, you're in a pressure cooker. It makes sense for athletes to focus on themselves. They're about to head into one of the most stressful, pressure-filled times of their lives. Everyone has their own stuff they're worried about. Yes, we're a team, but in many cases, we were also competing against each other. I didn't expect that everyone would have each other's back.

I liked hanging out with the older guys on the team—guys like Eric Vendt, Klete Keller, and Larsen Jensen. They were fun and supportive. Maybe it was just easier because they were guys and older; there was less competition. But they looked like they were having a good time. So they were who I tried to hang out with for the most part—with people who were positive and who treated me well. We played a lot of Risk in the team room, and that helped me feel more at ease.

We left Stanford and flew to Majorca, Spain, for more training and to get used to the time change before we went on to Athens. With all of my meets, I had traveled a lot in my life; however, traveling to Spain was my first time out of the country, and it would be both the farthest and the longest I'd ever been away. I would be out of the country without my parents and without my coach. Paul wasn't one of the Olympic coaches, so he wouldn't be with me. It felt disorienting. I was homesick.

Being away from my parents was maybe the hardest part. Talking to them helped keep me sane. The last time I'd seen them was in California, at the Olympic Trials in Long Beach, so when we talked, it was by phone. We all had cell phones in 2004, but this was before the days where you could just put a SIM card in your phone and make international calls. In order for me to call from Spain to Maryland I had to punch in a number that was on a prepaid calling card, and then go through a bunch of steps to put the call through to the U.S. We'd been in Majorca for a couple of days, and I was trying to call my mom and dad. I could not get the freaking phone to work. I broke down crying in the hallway. All I wanted to do was talk to my parents.

If you've read *The Hunger Games* or seen the movies, you have a little bit of an idea of what the Athens Olympics were like for me. The story is about this futuristic society where, to control the people living in the different districts, every year the government holds a competition that pits kids selected to represent their district against kids from other districts in a fight to the death. Before the competition, there's all this pomp and circumstance, and the kids are presented to the world as celebrities. The games are a huge event, and the whole nation watches. Then the kids go into the arena and proceed to try to kill each other. The last one alive wins.

Okay, at the Olympics no one dies, and no one's actually trying to kill anyone else, but for me, the experience in Athens in 2004 was isolating and terrifying. When I talk about it today, I'll often say what a wonderful time it was, but I'm not really telling the truth. If I'm totally honest, it was hard for me to escape the feeling of impending doom.

Fortunately, being an Olympian comes with perks that help distract you. Back in California, they took us into this massive room at a hotel where we got outfits from both USA Swimming and the U.S. Olympic Committee—shirts and pants and workout clothes, on and on. And you get to do that twice. In Athens, the cafeteria in the Olympic Village was awesome because there were stations with food of different nationalities, and you didn't have to pay for any of it. We also had a little key tag that we could punch to get free Coke from a machine. Instead of having to use money, the can just came out. When you're 15, all of this is very cool, sort of like Christmas. Our dorm rooms were pretty basic, though, and small. Dana Vollmer and I rearranged our room maybe three times trying to figure out a way to get more space. There was no way. There was no more space.

Being in the Olympic Village, you're around all these incredible athletes from other countries. In making the team, I was with people who had been my heroes. Here were these great swimmers that I had looked up to for so long, swimmers who had been on posters in my bedroom, and now I was teammates with them.

I skipped the opening ceremonies because I had to swim the 400-IM preliminaries the next day. The distractions of the Village were gone. I felt something in the pit of my stomach, and it didn't feel good. It was time to race.

***

Everything about Athens felt different. I wasn't in my own bed at night. I wasn't with my NBAC teammates. I wasn't with my coach. I wasn't going home at night to dinners that my mom cooked. There was nothing familiar for me to hang onto. You've heard the expression "attitude is everything?" Well, mine heading into my first event, the prelims for the 400-IM, was not great. I felt like I was falling in space with nothing to grab to stop my fall. I had won this race at the Olympic Trials six weeks earlier. That made me America's best hope. *Yeah, right. That seemed like so long ago.*

I saw my call time come closer and closer and just wished that time would stop so my prelim would never get here. Kaitlin Sandeno, who ended up winning silver in the 400-IM, and had inspired my Olympic aspirations four years earlier when she medaled in Sydney, tried to pump me up, "Let's go! Let's do it!" she said. But at that point, nothing anyone could have said to me would have helped. I was just too far gone. Instead of thinking about winning this race at the Olympic Trials, all I could think about was my prelim at trials, when I'd swum 10 seconds worse than my best time. That underwhelming race was what was stamped in my brain, and I could not get rid of it. It was around a hundred degrees out, and we were swimming in an outdoor pool. The sun bore down. I did not feel ready for what I was about to do.

In the 1900 Olympic Games, in Paris, a Dutch crew team of coxed pairs needed a coxswain. In coxed pairs, two people rowed while a third, the coxswain, yelled at them and told them what to do. (Olympic rowers would no doubt take exception to that description, but that's the way it looked.) The Dutch, who were favored to win, had rowed their preliminary race with a grown man as their coxswain, and they were soundly beaten by a French team whose far lighter coxswain was just a child. So for the final, the Dutch fired their adult coxswain, and found a young French boy to replace him. The Dutch went on to win the event in a close race, and the boy was photographed during the medal ceremony before he disappeared into the crowd. His name and his age have been lost to history, but people who have looked at the photo figure he's somewhere between seven and 12 years old.

If we assume the French boy was 12, then the youngest Olympic medalist was most likely a Greek gymnast who competed in 1896, also in Athens. (The 1896 summer games are called Games of the I Olympiad, as these games are considered to be the birth of the modern Olympics.) His name was Dimitrios Loundras, and he was 10 years and 218 days old. He finished third in the parallel bars, taking bronze. In 1896, third place in the parallel bars was also last place, as there were only three competitors. The youngest Olympic medalist to actually beat another competitor was an Italian girl named Luigina Giavotti, who won silver in team gymnastics in Amsterdam in 1928. She was 11 years and 302 days old.

I say all of this because by the standards of history, being a 15-year-old at the Olympics is really not all that big of a deal. Nadia Comaneci was 14, in 1976, when she won three gold medals and became the first Olympic gymnast to score a perfect 10.

Still, at 15 years old, I felt young. I *was* young, and my total lack of experience at international meets only added to my problems.

My race in the 400-IM prelims turned out to be a perfect storm—a disaster. Fearing a repeat of my subpar swim in the prelims of the Olympic Trials, where I'd gone out too fast, I tried to hold myself back. But I was expending energy holding myself back, when I should have been swimming relaxed and breathing relaxed like you're supposed to do at the start of the 400-IM. I was also stiff from trying so hard not to swim too fast too soon.

In the 400-individual medley you swim each of the four strokes for 100 meters, or two lengths each of a 50-meter pool. Butterfly comes first, then backstroke, breaststroke, and you finish with freestyle. When we made the turn from butterfly to backstroke, I lost all sense of where I was in the race. (Technically you're not supposed to look to see where the other swimmers are, but everyone does.) Granted, the first 200 meters of the race had never been my strength, but I could sense that the other swimmers were farther ahead of me than I wanted them to be. I fought, with limited success, not to let panic start to set in.

Breaststroke is one of my biggest strengths, but instead of feeling a surge of adrenaline at the turn from backstroke to breaststroke, I felt tapped out. I'd been swimming way too inefficiently, and now my body felt like Jell-O. I had nothing left to give. This created more panic, which led to hyperventilation, which led to catastrophe. I chopped and thrashed, struggling to get myself through the race without embarrassing myself too badly. As I swam my last 100 meters, I knew things were not going to end well. When I finally hit the wall, I barely had the energy to take my goggles off. The masochist in me couldn't resist looking at the clock. To my surprise, I hadn't swum as slowly as I had at the Olympic Trials prelim in Long Beach, but I'd still gone 10 seconds over my fastest time. I came into the Olympics ranked in the top eight, maybe even the top five in the world. People were saying I could medal in this event, possibly even win gold. But I finished sixth in my heat, and 17th overall. That meant I wouldn't swim in the finals.

You would think at this point that things could not have gotten any worse. You would be wrong. At the Olympics, you don't have time to stay in the pool and wallow, because the next heat is getting ready to start. So I pulled myself out, sprawled on the pool deck, and then threw up all over it. It can happen after lactic acid builds up after intense exercise. I remember photographers started to surround me, as if this were somehow newsworthy, and my coaches stepped in to try to shield the crumpled mess of me from them.

Jack Bauerle and Frank Busch, two of the Olympic coaches, came over to offer support. "Katie, it's going to be okay," one of them said. No, it wasn't okay. Memorable, maybe. Motivating, certainly, though I wouldn't understand that until later. But okay? Nope. Not even close. Nothing about this was okay.

Paul, my NBAC coach, was there, watching from the stands, but because he wasn't one of the official Olympic coaches, he wasn't supposed to be down on the pool deck. But at that point, with me doubled over and puking, people were like, "Poor girl. She feels awful. Maybe we should let her see her coach." So they got Paul a deck pass, and he was able to come out to me. He was very supportive. At that moment there probably wasn't one human being on the planet who could observe what I was going through and not be supportive. I was a 15-year-old girl having a meltdown. His advice was to go back to my room, get some rest, and regroup.

I take back what I just said. At that moment, maybe there was one human being on the planet who could see what I was going through and be less than supportive. One of the commentators—a former Olympic gold medalist and world record holder, one of the greatest women's swimmers ever, someone whose picture I had in my scrapbook—criticized me for having a bad attitude after losing, for not shaking people's hands or something. *Excuse me? I'm not shaking people's hands because I'm vomiting on the pool deck.* When I found out she'd said that I just started crying.

Retreat and regroup—those were about the only options open to me. In just two days, I had to swim the prelims of the 200-IM.

✶✶✶

Some of my teammates were great at this time. I remember Gary Hall Jr.—he's another swimming icon, with 10 Olympic medals, including a gold in the 50-freestyle in Athens—he gave me this little toy Army soldier. That's so like him. It was his way of saying, "Come on, you're a fighter, and you're a warrior. Don't let this get you down." That meant so much to me. Recently, when my husband Todd and I were packing up to move from Chicago to New York, I found that toy soldier. I'd kept it all those years.

Jason Lezak was another one. He has eight Olympic medals, but at that point—this was day one in Athens—he was not having a great meet. His message to me was that "This stuff happens—you have bad meets. You just gotta get back up." It's worth noting that Jason did a pretty good job of following his own advice. He left Athens with a gold, a bronze, and a world record, in the 4 x 100-medley relay.

In the Olympics, everyone is so caught up in what they are doing that it can be hard to find time to show compassion to others. That's what made what Gary and Jason did stand out so much. Sure, it might have been Jason's second Olympics, and Gary's third Olympics, so that might put them in a better position to offer support and advice. But to go out of their way to sit down and talk to someone who's having a hard time—there weren't a lot of people who did that.

Embrace the suck. They didn't use those words, but essentially that's what they were saying. The situation might be bad, but I would just have to deal with it.

✶✶✶

There are a ton of warm-up and warm-down pools in the pool area, and the next day Paul sat me down at one. He told me I had to put the 400-IM race behind me. "You gotta get back up," I remember him saying, echoing what Jason had said. He put me through a workout designed to make me feel good in the water. I don't think we did any pace work at all. He reminded me that I had trained enough to recover. That played to my strengths—if I'd done it before, I could do it again. Right then, I needed that. I needed him to hover. At that moment, I was a fragile, fragile girl who needed every amount of love and support possible. "Let's do it," we said.

And I sort of did. In the semifinals of the 200-IM, I won my heat. My time was more than a second slower than my best time ever, but still—I won my heat. And for maybe the only time at the Athens Olympics, I smiled. There's proof—a photographer caught it on camera.

I went into the finals ranked third, but I felt like I'd already given everything I had. I ended up finishing seventh. People would say, "Oh my God. You should be so proud. At 15, you're seventh in the world." I didn't feel proud. I felt the opposite of proud, like I'd let myself and the team down. I was supposed to go home with a medal.

✶✶✶

The 200-IM final was day four, which meant there were four more days of swimming. I wasn't swimming then, but I stayed in Athens for all of that time, and I tried to make the best of it. There were some pictures taken of me with some of my teammates where I was trying hard to look happy and supportive, but you could tell I wasn't having a good time.

Then there was some drama. There were more than 300 total events at the Athens Olympics, with over 10,000 athletes competing. After the swimming ended, there was another week of competitions in other sports. I wanted to stay. I wanted to see other sports. I wanted to stay for the closing ceremonies—I didn't know if I was ever going to be able to take part in another one. But the National Team director had other ideas—he decided that since I was so young, I should be sent home.

Everything everyone hears about the Olympics and the Village is 100 percent accurate. There are parties all over the place, many of them thrown by Olympic sponsors. All you have to do to get in is show your Olympic credentials, and then everything's comped. You hear about Olympic athletes whose relationships with girlfriends or boyfriends back home fall apart after the Olympics. Well, what happens in the Village is one of the big reasons. Looking back at it now, through the eyes of a woman in her early 30s, I can see why this might not have been a great environment for a 15-year-old girl out on her own. But in that moment, as that 15-year-old girl out on her own, I didn't see it that way at all.

I threw a fit. How dare they tell me I had to go home! I remember being on the team bus that shuttled us from the pool back to the Village, arguing my side of this gross injustice with Teri McKeever, who was one of the coaches. I have a lot of appreciation for how she responded. She just sat there and let me talk, and vent, but she listened to me. She could see how upset I was, but she listened, and that made me feel respected.

Eventually they decided I could stay—though with an insanely early curfew—but the next day I went to the head coach and said, "All right. I should go home." I missed home. It turned out that what this was really about was that I didn't want to be told I had to leave—I wanted it to be my decision.

The night swimming ended, I had my suitcases all packed. We had our team end-of-the-meet meeting, and we finished late, and then Paul had a great idea. We were in Greece. We were in Athens. We were in this very historic place that's so deeply embedded in Olympic history. But, aside from one day I had gone off on a little sightseeing venture with some teammates, I hadn't seen much of anything aside from the Olympic venues. He suggested that we go see the Acropolis. I checked out of the Village, and at around two or three in the morning he and I got a taxi and went there. I remember standing there on a hill above the city, looking at the Acropolis all lit up. It was really quite beautiful. I'm very glad we did that. I'm grateful to Paul for thinking of it.

Paul and I flew from Athens to Dulles Airport, outside of Washington, D.C. From there we took a van back to Abingdon. When I saw my mom, she burst into tears. My mom is not the kind of person who shows her emotions like that. She's even-tempered and a good analyzer. She would say that I swam the way I swam in Athens because I wasn't fully prepared for an Olympic stage. Well, I don't think we were prepared as a family, either. Everything happened so fast. I made the team. I was off to Stanford, and then Spain, and then Athens, all without them.

I understand why they didn't go. There are a lot of families in the world of competitive swimming with a lot of money. Ours wasn't one of them. We weren't poor, but we weren't rich, either—we were comfortably middle-class, and that meant my parents had to make financial sacrifices to support my swimming. I got that, and I will always be grateful for that. I wouldn't have wanted them to go into debt to come watch me swim in Athens. None of us ever dreamed it would turn out to be such a traumatic experience. None of us ever imagined they'd be sitting in their living room 5,000 miles away in Abingdon, Maryland, watching on TV while their daughter puked on the Olympic pool deck.

I watched the closing ceremonies from home.

THE HELL SET

Back in Abingdon, I took a week or so off—just stayed out of the pool and tried to regroup. The Abingdon NBAC team held a congratulations party for me at our house. I remember how nice and supportive it was—how everyone brought cards, and poured a ton of love out for me. I didn't have a great time at the party. To be honest, I felt kind of ashamed. I hadn't medaled, so I felt like I had failed.

After the party, it was, *okay, back to work.* It was time to prep for the 2005 World Championship trials—eight months away.

It wasn't long after I started working out again that Paul pulled me aside one day and told me about the Hell Set. The Hell Set was legendary set at NBAC—a workout that, when inflicted on an unfortunate swimmer, promised to be light years more demanding than any they'd ever done. He wouldn't tell me what it would entail (the Hell Set can get tweaked each time it's deployed), and he wouldn't tell me when I would do it. That was part of his point—this Hell Set cloud would just hang there over my head, and I wouldn't know when it would happen. When it did happen, I would just have to deal with that. I would have to "embrace the suck," in other words, though this particular suck figured to be bigger than previous sucks.

The anticipation was not at all fun. Every day I'd go to practice wondering, *is today going to be the day? Is today going to be the day?* I'd go home wondering, *is tomorrow going to be the day?* Then finally, one Friday morning, he told me that the day had arrived. It was time for the Hell Set. It was just Paul and me and the pool.

Paul's Hell Set was 8,000 yards of individual medley, and then on top of that I had to swim an 800-yard IM for time. I was exhausted when we finished, only to have him tell me that we hadn't finished. After I swam the 800, Paul had me warm down for 100 yards or so and then get back up on the blocks to swim another 200-yard IM for time. It was grueling, and it was painful, and it was just what I needed to rebuild my confidence. Part of the Hell Set was the swimming, but most of it was for my head, for the boost it gave my psyche to know that I could do something so hard and do it after weeks of anxiety wondering when the Hell Set would happen. Then it happened, and I did it. Performing when I had anxiety churning in my stomach wasn't my strong suit. But I was getting better at it.

FEAR

It grips and paralyzes. It feels like at any moment the ground beneath you is going to fall away. But it's also what makes something worth doing. Without fear, winning wouldn't be as valuable. I feared the 400-IM because of all the strategy that went into it and because of all the pain I knew I'd feel swimming it. It's the race I put the most pressure on myself to win, the one I most feared losing, and the race I felt I'd accomplished the most when I managed to win.

For me, fear and its close friend anxiety are constants. Even when things are going well, I know they're hanging out just around the corner. "Control the controllables," they say, and I try to live by that, but no matter how much I control, I'm always worrying that things will not work out the way I hope they'll work out. What if? I'm always asking myself, and in my mind the answer is never good. Todd, my husband, is good at staying calm and not overreacting in stressful situations. So when I think this way, it drives him crazy.

ON
SWIMMING
WELL

I'm not the most analytical swimmer in the world. I've taught swimming lessons, I've done a lot of swimming clinics, and I know how to improve a swimmer's technique to help them swim faster, but I don't think I'd be a great coach. I don't have the patience for it. I know what worked for me. Swimming always felt like a very natural habitat, unlike, say, running. When I run now, my husband, Todd, who played football in college at Michigan State, says I run like a swimmer, and that's not meant as a compliment. I'm knock-kneed. I don't have the proper support for my back and my hips. He says I'm wrecking my body. There are times when I feel super sore from running or lifting weights, and I want to grab a kickboard and get in a pool and just kick. It just feels good. It feels natural. I think most competitive swimmers would agree.

I don't swim much these days. It may sound strange to hear me say this, but I'd be lying if I said I just love to swim. When I was little I would say I loved swimming, but I loved it because it was a means to an end, a vehicle to get to a certain outcome, and it's the outcome I loved—competing, and especially winning—more than the swimming itself. I suppose it could have happened in another sport, like track and field (except, see above about my running), but it just happened to be swimming. I don't think this is an abnormal thing; there are a lot of swimmers who don't want to go near a pool after they stop competing. I'm enormously grateful that swimming provided me the ability to excel at something, but since I've stopped competing, the bloom has faded from that rose.

A big part of swimming well is body position. I don't remember ever consciously working on having good body position. It just came naturally to me, and I think this may be one of those areas where natural talent comes in to play. When you start swimming as a kid, you have to have a certain amount of strength and ability to pull and kick, but good body position is something that's hard to teach. If I'm watching someone swim, I know what to correct, and I can show someone what to correct, but there are limits to how much I can fix. Some people just get this naturally, they just position their bodies in the water better than others.

When I worked for Equinox, which is one of the top performance fitness organizations, I started a class called Swim Athletics. It was a 45-minute class, and participants had a range of skill levels. We had people who could barely swim 100 yards in two minutes, and we had people who could do that easily. One man in the class had an almost insane love for swimming. He even did private lessons with me. His work ethic was great. He would practice every single day, and he definitely got better. But his body rode so low in the water, and neither he nor I could understand why. I'd ask him about his hips and suggest that he tilt his pelvis a certain way. I'd look at him underwater to try to figure out what was going on. He was a good guy who wanted to be a better recreational swimmer. I gave him a full-force Olympian-style treatment, and I was able to help him drop his 100-yard times by five or 10 seconds. But he challenged my analytical abilities. Something wasn't quite right, something to do with his feel for the water, and ultimately, I couldn't figure out how to fix it. I wondered if it was just too late in life for him—that swimming was too foreign an activity for him, and maybe he had to have built some muscle memory earlier in his life. Or maybe he had great muscle memory, but what his muscles remembered were bad habits. I'm not an exercise physiologist, so I might be getting this totally wrong, but that was my interpretation.

If you want to swim competitively, it helps of course to have a good coach and to be coachable. You have to be able to hear a coach tell you to do something, and then execute it. Part of that involves swimming the sets and intervals you get assigned, but part of that is also technique. A lot of beginning swimmers struggle with the mechanics and timing of their breathing, and a coach can help with that, especially when you're young.

You also learn through repetition. When you do something the right way over and over, muscle memory kicks in, and it starts to become automatic. As the saying goes, it's not practice that makes perfect, but perfect practice that makes perfect. Here again, a good coach can help to cultivate good habits and weed out the bad ones.

When elite swimmers swim a workout, they typically go for about two or two-and-a-half hours. You might start with a warm up, and then do a speed set to get your heart rate up. Then you might move on to a kick set, followed by a main set—which could be very different for different swimmers and strokes—and then warm down to finish. The days may be different. Some days will be speed days, while others could be aerobic threshold days, or recovery days (if memory serves, those were rare). On days when you do doubles—two workouts, usually one early in the morning and the second in the afternoon—you might do more kicking and pulling in the morning, to set up something different for the afternoon.

People ask if we end up training a lot harder or differently in an Olympic year, and the answer is no, not really. We'd be doing the same sets. The general training format and structure doesn't change a whole lot; it's what you do with that structure. The effort level has to be there 100 percent of the time.

Beyond that, there are so many different coaching philosophies. Swimming can be very old school, and sometimes I think it lags behind some other sports. There can be this sense of, *okay, pound it out, let's get the yards in*. That's never worked well for me. It breaks my body down. So a lot of success depends on finding a coach and a style that works for you.

Granted, a lot of young swimmers don't have that option. It's like, *here's the club team near you, here's the coach, join or don't*. Those who join just have to play the cards they're dealt. The hope is that the swimmers with the most talent will rise up. The ones who don't rise up—well, maybe they're not talented enough, or maybe they're not putting in the work, or maybe they're locked into a situation with a certain club and a certain coach who's not best suited to their needs.

You can have the best preparation in the world and still, when you get in the pool, things can go wrong. People have made fun of me for this obsession I have with pressing my goggles into my eye sockets over and over before a race. Is that a little psychotic? Yes, but guess what? I have never had my goggles fall off or fill up with water in a major race. And it happens to the best of us. In the Beijing Olympics, in the finals of the 200-butterfly, Michael Phelps had his goggles fill with water. And he still won the race and set a world record doing it. Think of what he might have done if he'd been able to see!

At the Olympics in Athens, we competed in an outdoor pool, and when I swam the individual medley I had to adjust my stroke count coming into the backstroke turn because the flags they string over the pool (so you know how close you are to the wall) were blowing sideways. In Montreal for the World Championships, I misjudged the wall on a turn, and my weak push-off most likely cost me a spot in the finals. That's a correctable mistake, but I could never be 100 percent certain I wasn't going to make it again.

Is there such a thing as a perfect race? I used to get asked that a lot. I think there is. I feel like my 400-IM in the 2007 World Championships, when I set a world record, was a perfect race. I felt relaxed. I strategized well. Everything went as planned. I had what we call "easy speed." There's a thing in swimming that if you push something too hard, you can end up going slower. What you want to do is just let the adrenaline take you and achieve a fast time without over-expending either your physical or emotional energy. Some days you have it, and some days you don't. I don't know if it's even explainable by science. And "easy speed" is a lot easier to experience when you're in first place than when you're in fourth.

I've talked about "embracing the suck." That doesn't just mean to suck it up. It's not about passive acceptance of your situation. "Embrace the suck" means that to rise to the top in any field—swimming or track or business or whatever—you have to be willing to work really hard, and sometimes that work is going to be uncomfortable, or inconvenient, or unpleasant. And "embracing the suck" means accepting that sometimes, no matter how dedicated the embrace, you're going to fall short. But it doesn't mean you should never question how things are done. It doesn't mean that you shouldn't try to find a structure and a strategy that works best for you. I was fortunate as a young swimmer to have a coach who knew me, who could see what I was doing, and could dial things up or back as the need arose.

Success is a melting pot. It's a combination of talent, hard work, data, coaching, being able to handle pressure, and probably other things, luck included.

SWEAT

I don't notice sweat in the pool. Sweat is an indication that you're working hard, so it's strange that I don't notice it because in the pool I am definitely working hard. Now, when I work out in a gym, I feel badly if I don't sweat. I don't usually sweat when I lift weights, and that makes me question the quality of the workout, even though I know lifting is so good for me and good for how I look.

Outside a gym, sweat is just embarrassing. I always sweat at the airport. I'm not sure why. Because I'm stressed about making the flight, or anticipating hassles getting through security, or worried there might be turbulence? So when I go to the airport, I won't wear a colored shirt unless I can put a jacket over it. I don't want people to see sweat marks under my arms. I'm just vain in that way, and maybe in other ways, too. When I swam, I would wear earrings and eyeliner, and I hated being on the podium with my hair up. I liked to feel girly and pretty, and I hated the stereotype that jocks couldn't be cute.

Outside of sports, sweat means you've lost control, that you're not perfect, and, for better or worse, I've invested a lot of time trying to be perfect. Inside sports, it signals effort. Sweat is only acceptable when there's deep purpose behind it.

COMING BACK

After the disappointment of Athens, regaining my confidence was the number one priority. Paul was named the head coach of North Baltimore Aquatic Club, so in order to keep training with him, our family moved from Abingdon to Towson, not far from the main NBAC pool at the Meadowbrook Aquatic Center. Bob Bowman, NBAC's previous head coach and Michael Phelps's coach, took a job as head swimming coach at the University of Michigan, and Michael went to Michigan to work with him there. Michael had won eight medals in Athens, including six golds, and people began predicting even greater things for him. Mark Spitz's record of seven swimming gold medals in one Olympics had stood for 36 years, and there was speculation that Michael could break that record in 2008 in Beijing.

I buried myself in my training. I gained momentum in practice. I swam in a number of smaller meets and did well. That's what it took. There weren't any magic words that anyone could say to me—it was just day after day swimming strong paces and getting strong results.

My confidence grew. Not long after the Olympics I swam in Indianapolis at the 2004 Short Course World Championships.

They'd put a pool on the floor of the Conseco Fieldhouse, where the Indiana Pacers play, so the environment was pretty awesome. I won a silver in the 400-IM and a bronze in the 200-IM in front of an energetic and supportive crowd. It sounded like thunder when you walked out on the pool deck. We may have been in Indianapolis, but this was the *World* Championships, and some of the best swimmers from all over the planet were there, so those were my first international medals.

Paul Yetter and I at Meadowbrook post-practice. We had just returned from the 2004 Short Course World Championships in Indianapolis. I am proudly wearing my first-ever international medal.

Success built on success. In April 2005, I was back in Indianapolis for the trials for the Long Course World Championships. I won the 200 and 400-IM and broke my first ever American record in the 200-IM. That feeling of redemption and vindication rose up, and I felt so proud. Michael gave me the biggest hug after my race. The electric pink iPod shuffle my parents let me purchase as a reward was icing on the cake. I won the 200-freestyle, and I also made the team in the 200-backstroke. We had three months until the 2005 World

Championships in Montreal, but I was successfully putting the frustrations of Athens behind me. Every star was aligning. Everything that I wanted to happen was happening.

Then I hit a little bump in the road. We were back in Baltimore, and for some reason at one of our workouts we started out wearing fins. It wasn't something we normally did, but I didn't think too much about it. But I didn't warm up, and I started fast. After the workout I felt a sharp pain on top of my foot. I had strained a tendon. I tried to ignore it, but after a couple of days it had gotten worse, so my mom took me to a foot doctor.

He examined my foot and said I'd have to wear a boot for eight weeks. Eight weeks! I thought, *it's 12 weeks until the World Championships, so there's no way I can wear a boot for eight weeks.* My mom agreed with me, and we got up and left. She took me home and we treated it with less restrictive things like salves with arnica and comfrey, which were supposed to be good for bruising and swelling. I didn't kick in the pool for 10 days. I was beside myself, freaking out. I'd had minor injuries, but this felt more serious, and until now everything had been going so well. Fortunately, I still had plenty of time, and at 16, I healed fast. I got better, but the whole experience scared me.

My foot injury turned out to not be a problem at the World Championships in Montreal. I won the 200-and 400-IM. We also won our 4 x 200-freestyle relay. These were my first gold medals in long course international competition. The U.S. team did well too. We finished first in the medal standings with 39 medals, 17 of them gold.

Watch my first World Championship title!

I didn't make the finals of the 200-freestyle, so that was one disappointment, and there was some weirdness associated with that. When I was warming up, Klete Keller, on the men's team, came up and asked if he could borrow my pull buoy. "Sure," I said. "Fine. No problem." So I let him borrow it. When I swam the semifinal for the 200-free, I didn't have a great race. I had the ninth best time, which meant I didn't qualify for the finals. After the race, Paul was angry. He said that lending Klete my pull buoy destroyed my focus and ruined my race. Mind you, this was after I'd just won my first World Championship final, in the 200-IM. So here I'm having the best meet of my life, and he's blaming my one slip-up on a piece of swimming equipment I loaned to a friend?

This may have been the first time I really pushed back at him. I told him lending Klete the pull buoy had nothing to do with the race, and he was out of line for suggesting it did. I knew exactly what had happened in the 200-free. I had a bad turn at the third wall, and that cost me a few tenths of a second, and those few tenths of a second put me in ninth place. It was as simple as that. I called my mom and told her I was so confused, that I didn't understand why Paul would make such a big deal out of something that I was sure had no bearing on the race. I learned later, years later, that he called my mom while we were in Montreal and told her he was upset that I wasn't focusing enough on him, that I wanted to hang out with my teammates instead. You can't really fly red flags in swimming pools, but one had gone up in our relationship.

✷✷✷

I had turned 16 in June of 2005, and in September, after the World Championships, I got to fulfill one of my other Olympic goals. Nearly every Olympian I know has gotten a tattoo of the Olympic rings. At 15, right after Athens, I was too young to get mine. But once I turned 16, I could get one with my parents' consent, and my parents consented. This had been a dream of mine. I may not have raced the way I'd hoped I'd race in Athens, but I was still an Olympian, and I was proud of that.

I've always had a sort of paranoia about coming off as too cocky, so when I got the tattoo, I wanted to hide it a little bit. I got it on the right side of my lower back—upper butt, I guess you could say—and I purposely picked that spot because I didn't want it on my wrist, or my ankle, or anywhere where it could be seen. The only time you could see it was when my swimsuit got pulled up to the side. I didn't want to draw attention to it. I didn't want people to ask me about it. I just got it for me.

My mom, who researches everything, researched tattoo parlors, a fact that should go in the "above and beyond" section of mothering manuals. She found a really good, clean place. I waited until after Worlds because I had to stay out of the pool for a week, so that meant finding a time when I'd be able to do that. There are five interlocked rings—blue, black, and red on the top and yellow and green underneath. "These five rings represent the five parts of the world now won over to the cause of Olympism and ready to accept its fecund rivalries," the founder of the modern Olympics, Pierre de Coubertin, is believed to have said, making the Olympics sound like some kind of disease. The Olympic Charter says the rings are supposed to represent the "union of the five continents." Of course, there are seven continents. Antarctica doesn't have teams, so that makes six. The Olympics' founders seemed to be counting differently. My yellow ring started fading immediately, and I had to get it touched up in 2009.

TURNING PRO

Near the end of the 2005 season, I decided to become a professional swimmer. It wasn't an easy decision. On the one hand, I was finishing my most successful year ever, and there figured to be several more successful years on the horizon. If all worked out, these could be the most financially lucrative years of my life. So it made sense to capitalize on that success, turn pro, and earn some money. On the other hand, I was 16. I would graduate from high school in a year and a half, then go to college. Turning pro meant I would lose my eligibility to swim on a college team. I had heard a lot from friends who had swum in college about how great the team experience was, how supportive it could be to have a tight-knit network of teammates. I sort of thought I could get that kind of experience from being on Team USA, but it really wasn't the same. Though turning pro didn't mean I would miss out on the experience of going to college—the contract Speedo offered me included paying for my college education—it just meant I wouldn't be able to swim on a college team.

In the end, I figured I was going to be going after the same goals regardless—world records, Olympic medals—so I might as well get compensated for it. Also, swimming is an expensive sport. Swimsuits alone, at the upper levels of the sport, can cost hundreds of dollars, and you only wear one a few times before you need a new one. (A slightly old suit means extra sag, which means a slower time, and that slower time, even if it's only by fractions of a second, can mean the difference between first place and last place.) Then there's travel, and all the costs associated with that. I liked the idea that I could make money so my parents wouldn't have to pay for everything. I liked that they wouldn't have to worry about paying my college tuition. And I liked that I would still be able to put some money away for my future. My parents didn't pressure me one way or the other. If anything, they were more worried than I was about the kind of pressure turning pro might create. But the more I thought about it, it just made a lot of sense.

I signed a 10-year deal with Speedo, which at the time was the longest contract they'd ever signed with an athlete. I had a choice between base pay at a certain level, or a lower base with the opportunity to earn higher pay if I hit certain performance benchmarks. I chose to go with the performance benchmarks. If all went according to plan, I'd be a Speedo swimmer at the 2008 Olympics in Beijing, the 2012 Olympics in London, and maybe even the 2016 Olympics in Rio de Janeiro. (As we'll see, all did not go according to plan. But we're getting ahead of ourselves.)

Before I signed with Speedo, I signed a contract with the sports marketing agency Octagon to represent me. Peter Carlisle became my agent. Peter's a brilliant guy who's responsible for much of the financial success I've had in my career, including negotiating my contract with Speedo and setting up my arrangements with other sponsors. In addition to Peter, my Octagon team included Drew Johnson, who helped me learn how to handle press conferences and media interviews, and Marissa Gagnon (now Marissa Fortier), my manager, whose wise counsel and friendship remain valuable to this day.

Shortly after I turned pro, a story on the ESPN website quoted Sheree Watson, then president of Speedo North America. "Every once in a while, a special athlete comes along who demands a special commitment," she said. "Katie's versatility and raw talent give her the potential to achieve great accomplishments along the same lines as Michael Phelps." It wasn't the first, and it wouldn't be the last time I would hear that comparison.

Part of being a pro swimmer for Speedo obviously meant wearing their racing suits. That wasn't going to be hard to do. I'd been using Speedo suits for years. The only difference was that now Speedo was paying for them. It was also in my contract that I had to do about a dozen appearances for them—clinics, speeches, a couple of photo shoots, things like that. Speedo gave me a fair amount of flexibility with those, understanding that I had a training schedule and trying not to interrupt it too much.

My first Speedo photo shoot. I was so nervous. (Photo by Michael Muller)

At one of my first photo shoots, in a studio in Los Angeles, the photographer told me he was good friends with Joaquin Phoenix, the actor. At one point he told me to turn around, so he could get a shot of my butt, so he could send it to Joaquin. I was wearing a bikini. It feels really strange looking back on it now, but at the time I was 16, and I didn't think it was strange and I didn't feel uncomfortable.

That stuff just happened. I went out to dinner that night with some people from Speedo, and we laughed about it—it was sort of a joke. I didn't think anything of it. Even now looking back I'm not upset or troubled by it. It's just—wow. That's how things operated, and I didn't even think anything of it, which is crazy.

When I turned pro, people warned me about other things. They wanted me to know that turning pro could change swimming from a sport that was fun to something that was now a job. I remember thinking, *yeah, but, whether I'm a pro or not, I already see swimming as being sort of like a job.* And I don't mean that in a bad way at all. I figured, *why not get paid for something that I'm already so intense about?*

At that time, even if you weren't a professional, there were certain meets where they awarded money. After the Athens Olympics, but before I turned pro, I got a check in the mail for $10,000 for my seventh place finish in the 200-IM. I had never seen a check for that much money. It meant being able to take my friends out for sushi or go shopping and buy shirts for my brother or my boyfriend. All of that was so fun. Money didn't ruin anything—it motivated me. With Speedo and the incentives in my contract, I thought, *all right, if I hit this pace or break this record, I get this amount of money.* And that would psych me up. I was riding high and crushing things in the pool.

My contract was nearly 30 pages long, and to be honest, I didn't have a ton of input into the details of it. I trusted my dad, Peter, and a lawyer we hired. But even though I was less than intimately aware of much of the contract, I understood how my performance incentives worked. For example, if I went under 1:56 for the 200-meter freestyle, I would get a $50,000 bonus. That's a lot of money when you're 16. (That's a lot of money at any age.) And I did that a bunch of times. The incentive structure could work against me, too. In 2009, when I didn't make the World Championship team, my contract got cut in half. But choosing performance incentives mostly worked out in my favor. I liked the risk and I liked the exhilaration of knowing that if I hit a certain threshold, I would get paid a lot.

I don't think I understood how "not normal" this all was. People were aware that I'd turned pro—it wasn't a secret. But I didn't talk about it much with anybody. I still don't today, except maybe with my husband. He'll remind me that it was insane for a 16-year-old to be making the kind of money I was making.

You hear a lot of stories about athletes, and in particular female athletes, who achieve a great deal of success in their sport at a really young age, and then you learn how domineering their parents were in their relationships with them. I want to go on record here as saying that I had—and have—great parents. They were tremendously supportive without ever being overbearing. My mom's strength to this day has been to look at my struggles and my successes and offer a reasoned perspective on them. She was the rock, the person I would call whenever I was freaking out about something. She could see all sides of things, even if sometimes that would drive me nuts. I'd think, *can you please just see things my way, and not give me both freaking sides of*

everything? Can you please just get excited for me? Now I realize how valuable her perspective was. She helped me get an outlook on things so I could make the best decision possible.

My dad was the one who would get excited. I would come home and tell him the times I'd swum in practice, or how close I was to one record or another, and he'd get all jazzed up. He was the hype man. This started early. I can't tell you how many times I've heard the story of him seeing me swim the 25-yard backstroke in a race when I was maybe five years old. His eyes would light up, and he would recount how I "just shot straight as an arrow down the pool." I've "shot straight as an arrow" down that pool so many times, you'd think I was Robin Hood. If I had a dollar for every time I've heard him tell that story, I'd be a zillionaire. If my mom was the wise counselor, my dad was more like my number one fan.

My dad and I at the NBAC Gala prior to the 2004 Olympic Trials.

I think parents of kids who are athletes are always wondering what they should be doing. My advice would be to let the kids take the lead. Don't push too much. My parents just rode the wave. They were there when I needed them, and they were great with logistics—helping me get to practice on time, making sure we always had hotels when we traveled, my mom bringing her little mini-stove to cook pasta when we were on the road. But they let me be in charge, or at least be in charge to the extent it made sense when I was a kid. They let me make mistakes. They let me figure out things for myself. They never pushed their own agenda.

After I turned pro, some of the decisions I made about my money—and remember, it was my money—would drive my father nuts. It's not like he or my mom ever thought some of it should be going to them. It was never that. It's that my value system at 16 about how to spend money wasn't exactly in sync with my dad's as an adult.

For example, at 16, I had my driver's license, and right off the bat I wanted to get a BMW. That was my dream. But my parents said no—that was too much car for a kid my age. Okay, fair point. They made me "settle" for an Audi A3. They didn't even let me get the regular Audi sedan—I had to get the dorkier hatchback. I still really liked it—what kid my age wouldn't like to have her very own brand new Audi? But it just didn't achieve the level of cool that I was shooting for.

My dad hated that I got a new car. It just went against every fiber of his being. He hated that I didn't spend months doing research and then buy a super reliable used car. I said no to that. I said a new car is what I want. I can pay for it. And so, boom! I did.

I can appreciate that saying all of this makes me sound like some sort of model, not just of Speedo swimsuits, but of a spoiled, elitist teenager. I can appreciate that not many 16 year olds would complain about having to "settle" for a new Audi. But no one was giving things to me for free. I was earning them. I had a job, and it paid me well. I understood that. And besides, driving the Audi to swimming practice wasn't really going to make me stand out. Sure, it was a nice car, but a lot of kids drove nice cars. And the Audi didn't have the cool factor that a BMW would have—especially a hatchback. And like I've said, a lot of kids in the swimming world come from families where there's a fair amount of money. The only thing that was different was that I was earning mine. Though that wasn't something I advertised.

Everything I bought seemed to have the potential to drive my father crazy. I remember once in Los Angeles I won a big race and I wanted to go out and buy a Chanel purse as a reward to myself. But it drove him up the wall that I would spend a lot of money on a designer purse. It just killed him.

"Dad hates this," I said to my mom, speaking not specifically about the Chanel purse, but about my newly earned capacity to buy nice things. And she knew. I think there were so many times that she had to talk him down and remind him that it was my money. Her argument with him was that I was seeing value in the things I spent money on, and that just because he didn't see value in those things didn't mean I shouldn't buy them. That was how I wanted to treat myself. I can't even imagine how those conversations went. Though it wasn't like I was being totally frivolous. I was living at home. I was putting money away. We were making smart investments toward my future.

In a strange way, knowing how much it aggravated him almost made me feel happy—I don't know why. Or maybe I do know why. Did I mention I was 16?

With my younger brother, it was different. Christian is three and a half years younger than I am, and at times the "professional swimmer" me could be a real pain in the ass to him. There was a popular Italian ice place near where we lived called Rita's. If he'd want to go, and it was raining, I'd say, "Okay, I'll drive you there, and I'll pay for it, but you have to get out of the car to buy whatever we get."

And so he would resent the conditions, resent that I was ordering him around, resent that I was flaunting my money, resent the whole situation as he walked up and got our Italian ices, and then came back to sit, resentfully, in the passenger seat of (my) car. I would do things like that just to annoy him.

Christian at 2½, and me at age 6.

But other times we'd go to the mall and I would tell him to just get whatever he wanted, and he would let me buy him clothes. I loved being able to do that.

I made a deal with my parents that if I set a world record, I could get the car I wanted. It took me two years, but in 2007, after I broke the world record in the 400-IM, I drove a new BMW right out of the showroom.

✶✶✶

I went through 2006 wide-eyed. It was a whole different world for me—doing photo shoots and swimming clinics and having people stand in line so I could autograph cards for them. I signed with some other sponsors—Omega (watches), Rosetta Stone (language learning), Playtex Sport (tampons) and Visa, and they all were very good to me, in terms of financial support and other perks. Omega gave me really nice luxury watches every year that I would regift to others. Visa sent me gift cards with my picture on them. Playtex empowered girls and women in sports. Very adult things were happening to me, and I was kind of blown away by it all. But at the same time, I was aware that all of these things were happening because of what I was doing. And knowing that only made me more focused and more motivated. If I kept swimming well, all these good things would keep happening, and I loved that. Pavlov's dogs would have understood.

So I kept training hard. Every day I went to practice, Paul gave me a master list where he'd recorded all of my best times. And it wasn't just my best times at the normal swimming events, but included things like my best time for a 25-yard breaststroke kick, or my best time for a 75-yard back/breast/free. His list was maybe 10 pages long, and I was absolutely obsessed with it. Any time he gave me a time I had to beat, I would beat it and then go home after practice and update the list. For me, a person who likes precision, it was very addicting.

At the clinics I do today it's not uncommon for coaches to want me to tell their swimmers about all the sacrifices that come with being a serious athlete. I have a hard time with this one. What I really want to say to them is "If what you're trying to accomplish is important enough to you, it doesn't feel like a sacrifice." If I would go out with friends on Saturday night, I would still get up at 7 a.m. on Sunday morning because there's practice at 8 a.m. and because that's just normal—it's not a sacrifice. That's what I needed to do in order to reach the goals I'd set for myself. It wasn't hardship—it was how I was going to get from where I was to where I wanted to be. If you see the work as a negative—as a sacrifice—it's going to be that much harder for you to become great at what you do. Conversely, if what you're aiming for means enough to you, then you're going to do the work. But it's got to be something you want—not just something your parents want, or your coaches want. If it's a grind to drag yourself out of bed to do the thing, then maybe it's not the right thing for you.

My first year as a professional swimmer worked out well for me in the pool. I got four firsts, a second, and a third at the Short Course Nationals in spring 2006. In early August, at the Long Course Nationals in Irvine, California, I took first place in the 200- and 400-IM and second in the 200- and 400-freestyle. Later that month, at the Pan Pacific Championships in Victoria, Canada, I got two golds—in the 200-freestyle and 400-IM—and two silvers, in the 400-freestyle and 200-IM.

BOYS

It's probably ironic that the years when I was swimming the fastest I had ever swum were also the years when I was experiencing the most drama in my personal life. Or maybe it's not ironic at all and is simply being a teenage girl, a time when drama seems to come with the territory.

Some of this drama got stirred up because of my relationship with Paul. Paul was probably the best coach I ever had. He understood me, understood what I needed from him, and what I needed to do in practice in order to excel. He understood my need for precision, and how just being told to swim harder wasn't going to cut it. I needed times, intervals, and measurable goals. He gave me those things. He was a great coach for me at a time when I needed someone to do exactly what he did. The results bear that.

But there was another side to things. There may be some athletes who are okay with having their coaches also be their good friends, but that wasn't going to work for me. I was 16 when we moved to Baltimore. When you're homeschooled like I was, you don't have a school social network to rely on, so most of my friends were on the NBAC team. These were my peers. They were my age. We liked to hang out together. They would invite me to homecoming and school dances, things you don't have when you're homeschooled. Paul was 13 years older than me. I wanted him to be my coach, but I didn't need him to also be my best friend. And I'm not at all sure those two roles—coach and friend—work very well together. Or maybe it wasn't so much that he wanted to be my friend, as it was that he thought that to get the best results in the pool he needed to exert a lot of control over me. I don't know. What I do know is that I was a normal 16-year-old girl wanting to do normal 16-year-old girl things. I wanted to be social and have friends and hang out with them after practice. I wanted to start dating boys. Those things pulled me away from Paul, and I think he had a hard time with that.

This played out in a number of ways. Before we moved to Baltimore, when we were practicing at Knight Diver in Abingdon, I didn't have a lot of friends, so I would spend more time interacting with him. Besides, he was the first coach I ever had who was coaching me to make an Olympic team, so at the start it all just made sense.

After we moved to Towson, this changed. I made friends, I had a social group, and the more time I wanted to spend with my friends, the less time I had for Paul. A sort of tug-of-war started. Sometimes Paul would keep me for an hour or more after practice to have these poolside chats. My teammates would call them our "Take Over the World" talks, and we'd talk about the medals I could win and the records I could set. Meanwhile my mom would be home with dinner ready thinking, *where are you? Why aren't you home?* I just wanted to get home and eat. I had just worked out for hours.

Or he'd be upset about my evening plans on weekends after a late practice, telling me not to stay out past 11 p.m. And I'd be infuriated. In 2006, I was 17 years old. It wasn't like I was going out drinking. I was maybe going over to a friend's house to watch a movie. The next day he would want to know what time I got home.

Or at meets after races I'd be with the other swimmers or texting my mom in the stands, and he would be mad that I was focusing on other people and not talking to him. *Was he jealous?* It sure seemed that way. There were always these little battles going on. I wanted him to be my coach, and that was it.

I want to be very clear about one thing. It takes only a quick Google search to find stories about male swimming coaches who have abused the girls they were coaching. USA Swimming was one of the first sports governing bodies to start publishing a public list of coaches and other officials who have been banned from coaching for violating its code of conduct. That list has more than 180 names on it, and the vast majority are there because of sexual abuse.

That never happened with Paul. That's a line that was never crossed, nor even approached. I just think he wanted more control over me than I was willing to give him. And that pressure could make me feel uncomfortable. I'm prepared to assume that his motive for wanting more control over my life came from the purest of places—from his desire to see me perform at the highest levels in the sport. In that sense, well, mission accomplished—2006 and 2007, when this pressure sort of reached a crescendo, were my best years ever as an athlete. But that wasn't because I ceded total control to him. I didn't. Maybe it's more that all these things going on in my life—having a group of friends to do things with, the drama with Paul—provided enough necessary distractions so I wasn't thinking about records and medals all the time. That would have driven me crazy.

For me the biggest issue with Paul was just his lack of trust. I'd been with him for four years, and that was long enough for him to understand that I was able to laser focus on improving as an athlete. So what if I had a life outside of the pool? He was my swimming coach. When it came to swimming, I was going above and beyond in everything he asked of me. Shouldn't that be enough?

Things got even more complicated when I started dating, as if dating when you're a teenager isn't complicated enough on its own. I suppose technically I went on my first date when I was in eighth grade, but that whole experience was a mess, and I broke it off quickly, so I don't think we can even count that. My first real date was when I was 16, with Nico Zebley. He was another swimmer, of course, and he swam at NBAC. Relationships among swimmers are pretty common. Swimmers are the people you're around day in and day out. That was even more true in my case, because I was homeschooled and didn't have classmates I spent time with. I think in my entire dating history, I probably only went out with two or three people who weren't swimmers. (It probably says something that I married one of them.)

With Nico, it wasn't love or anything. I was very naive, and he was very respectful of the fact that I'd never really dated before. He was just a very nice guy. I'm not sure if we were ever officially boyfriend and girlfriend, though he was the first boy I kissed. We went out on a few dates, and that was it. We just moved on and went our separate ways, and though I can't say for certain what was going on in his mind, it didn't feel awkward for me at all.

Relationships between swimmers can sometimes get pretty dicey. Our senior group was a small group. There would be all the flirting, all the game-playing, and all the normal things that you'd expect to happen with any relationships among teenagers. With such a small group, any coupling comes with a lot of potential for jealousy or hurt feelings. After you break up with someone, you're still on a team with that person, so you're still spending a lot of time together. And that person might now be dating somebody else on the team. It's called "swim-cest" for a reason, and it's a textbook formula for how problems can develop.

I met Dan Madwed in 2006. He was from Connecticut but relocated to Baltimore so he could swim with NBAC. For part of the time he was in Baltimore, Dan was also homeschooled, and we ended up spending a fair amount of time together. He would come over to my house before practice. I liked him, and I'm pretty sure he knew that I liked him, though I felt like he sort of dangled that knowledge in front of me. It was half a year to a year before he actually asked me out.

We had probably been "together" for several months before we made things official. It happened during the 2007 World Championships in Melbourne. Dan wasn't on the World Championship team, but he had flown to Australia because he made the team for what's called a Duel in the Pool, which is a country vs. country event between two countries that are among the best in swimming. In 2007 it was the U.S. vs. Australia, held in Sydney after Worlds. Dan and I were sitting in a corner of the team room one day in Melbourne. He asked me if I wanted to go out with him, meaning him exclusively.

I said yes, which meant we were officially dating, though at the moment I was single-minded bordering on psychotic in wanting to keep my focus on what I was in Melbourne to do, and that was to swim. The next day was the finals of the 400-IM, so I remember thinking, *okay, don't focus too much on Dan right now—you need to think about tomorrow.*

Paul didn't want me dating. He would tell me that my relationships with boys were going to hurt my swimming. This theme would play out over and over. At one point he and my mom even went out for coffee, and she told him to back off— that it was perfectly normal for me to have a boyfriend in my life.

Meanwhile, in Melbourne, the next day, I broke my first world record in the 400-IM. I had spent the whole meet watching people break world records and feeling that I wasn't allowed into an exclusive club. Then I did it, I conquered the event that had conquered me in Athens, in 2004. People have asked me what it's like to break a world record. Well, you can tell by my reaction at the end of the race. I leapt out of the water, feeling relief, pure happiness, and pride after three years of hard work. All of the pain that went into a 400-IM melted away. It was one of the highest highs of my career.

Watch the end of the race!

They teach you in school that there's correlation, and there's causation, and they are two different things. Correlation is when things tend to happen together, like formalizing my relationship with Dan one day and then setting a world record the next. Causation would say that the one—the relationship—caused the other—the world record—to happen. I'm inclined to file the dating and the record-setting into the folder labeled "correlation." And if Paul was going to raise questions about my relationships, then I was determined to show him that I could date and still swim my best. I would use it as fuel, as a way of saying, "Oh yeah? Just watch this!" Though I suppose you could say that pushes everything closer to the realm of causation.

So now Dan and I were dating and in this pressure-cooker. We were both trying to swim our best. Dan was trying to make an Olympic team. Paul was not loving the fact that we're dating, and Paul was Dan's coach, as well as mine. This all seemed pretty unfair to Dan, who was just trying to be a normal 16- or 17-year-old guy and dealing with everything that came with that. Though I guess the same applied to me as a 16- or 17-year-old girl.

Dan would come over to my house an hour or so before practice. We would hang out watching TV, laughing and talking about something that happened at practice the day before. And then we went to practice together. Paul would glare at us. I assumed, that he assumed, that because we came in together, other things must be going on. My attitude was, *yes, I'm dating this guy, but no, I'm not going to be late to practice, and no, I'm not going to let it affect my swimming.* I had seen girls get to the point where they would let a guy distract them. I wasn't going to let that happen to me, and I took it to the point of obsession. If Dan was going to hang out with me, then we were going to show up at practice early. We laughed and joked and everything, but I was still going to get my work done, no matter what. That was always my mentality. But Paul did not like that Dan had entered my life. I think he even talked to Dan about it, saying that this was a big year for me, and he shouldn't screw it up. I was very aware that we were being observed. Paul asked me questions about my relationship with Dan that he had no business asking. "It hasn't affected my swimming," I told him, "so please stay out of it."

If I step back and try to see things from Paul's perspective, I can understand that his concerns weren't coming from nowhere. He had seen other swimmers—other NBAC swimmers, other girl NBAC swimmers—deal with complications in their lives by spending a lot of time hanging out with boys. This contributed to negative consequences in performance and spirit. I think he may have been projecting that onto me, this idea that boys are trouble, and I should stay away from them. So in that context, he was just trying to be protective, or overprotective, maybe. And all of this may have had something to do with the fact that I came to him when I was 14 or 15 years old—when I was ready to follow whatever he said like some sort of robot. Now I was becoming an independent, young adult, and experiencing all the normal things that came with that.

✱✱✱

The relationship with Dan fizzled. I won't go into details, but later he told me it had to do with him feeling competitive with where I was in my career. Anyway, like most relationships that develop with people at a young age, it didn't work out. From the time we made it "official," it lasted maybe four months.

This brought Brennan Morris into the picture. Brennan was another NBAC swimmer, and I'd always been friendly with him. He liked to joke around and had a great sense of humor. He just made me feel good. Even before I broke up with Dan, when Dan was away, Brennan and I hung out a lot.

When I started dating Brennan, it caused friction between him and Dan. It was a very challenging time. I was a mess. I cried a lot. But then at the same time, I still swam the best I'd ever swum. I was determined that the drama in my personal life was not going to hurt my swimming, and it never did. When the tumult was about at its height of tumultuousness, in December 2007, I broke four American records in one meet in Annapolis at the Naval Academy—in the 200- and 400-yard IM and the 500- and 1000-yard freestyle. In some way, even with all the drama, and as messy as everything was, I think all of this made me feel normal. These guys were both people who I cared about. Having a boyfriend and going out on dates—these were normal things for a girl my age to do.

Things remained tense for all three of us—me, Dan, and Brennan—up to and even after the 2008 Olympic Trials. Dan and Brennan weren't talking to each other, but when I made the Olympic team Dan wished me good luck in Beijing. We were cordial at that point, but it was definitely awkward. When I got back from Beijing, Dan went off to the University of Michigan, so I didn't really have any connection with him after that.

✶✶✶

There was another male swimmer from Baltimore who had a significant influence on my life around this time, though not because we were dating or ever had any kind of boyfriend-girlfriend relationship. That person was Michael Phelps. Michael had come home from the Athens Olympics with eight medals, six of them gold. In the lead-up to the Beijing Olympics, he was the focus of a media barrage that was so overwhelming that it feels like it's downplaying it to call it unprecedented. Predictions were that he could win eight golds in Beijing, breaking Mark Spitz's record of seven and becoming the greatest swimmer of all time. I came home from Athens with zero medals, but after Athens I was on a tear, winning races and setting records. I was a world champion. Comparisons were inevitable, and to be honest, I didn't do a lot to discourage them. We swam for the same club. We were both at the top of our game. In fact, the *New York Times* headline read, "If you're looking for the next Michael Phelps, she's already in the pool."

Michael and I sharing a laugh at the 2008 Olympic Trials.

GREAT
EXPECTATIONS

You have to believe in yourself in order to reach your goals, especially if you set the bar high for those goals. But it's not at all unusual to also experience self-doubt. It makes us...what? More human, maybe? I've always struggled to find the right balance between the two, and this was never truer than in the months leading up to the 2008 Olympics in Beijing.

In late 2007 and into 2008, I had probably the highest level of self-confidence and the lowest level of self-doubt I'd ever had. I had the American record in the 200-freestyle. I was very close to the American record in the 200-IM. I had the world record in the 400-IM from April of 2007 until Australia's Stephanie Rice took it away from me it in the spring of 2008, and I took it back from her a few months later. I was ranked in the top two in the nation in five different events. If ever there was a time for me to feel hyperconfident about my ability to win any race I got into, this was it.

It's a lot easier for me to say that out loud now, more than a decade later, than it would have been in 2008. I remember doing press conferences leading up to the 2008 Olympic Trials, and I'd tell reporters how happy I would be just to make the Olympic team, how that alone would be such an honor. They would ask if I was already thinking ahead to Beijing, and I would say no—that I was just going to try to swim my best and take it one race at a time, and whatever happened would happen. But while I was saying that at that time, inside I was also thinking, *okay, you really do have this. You are going to win, and there's a good chance you're going to set a record doing it.* But even at this time of peak confidence, there was this fight going on in my mind between Katie "the self-assured swimmer" and Katie "the never-ending self-doubter." While one part of me would be telling myself, *girl, you have this!* Another part would jump right in and ask, *but do you?*

I'm a little envious of people who just overflow with confidence, and who can present themselves in that way too. They would go into a race saying, "Oh, yeah—I'm going to win this!" And maybe that's a reasonable and normal thing to do when all of your past experience gives you a good reason to overflow with confidence. Heading into 2008, my past experience did just that. But that wasn't me. I could never say something like that. Even thinking about it today, sends shivers down my spine. I could believe it inside, maybe. I might be able to say something like that to my parents, but they were probably the only ones I could say it to. I wouldn't even say it to Paul, because he was already amping things up enough without my adding to it. Maybe he could mark five different events down for me on a workout sheet and put GOLD, GOLD, GOLD, GOLD, GOLD next to them, but I could never be confident that was going to happen. I think that drove Paul crazy. I think to him it meant I didn't believe in myself. But that was just me. I just couldn't shake that little cloud of doubt out of my head.

My approach was to control what I could control. That's why I worked so hard in training. I used my training to convince myself of what I could do in competition. If I'd hit certain benchmarks in practice, then I would have every reason to exert confidence going into a meet. Maybe not 100 percent confidence, but close. In every race there are variables you can't control. I can't control what my competitors are going to do. Someone could always pull out something crazy.

Twice a year, in March and December, NBAC would swim a meet at Annapolis, at the Naval Academy. In March 2008 we went there, and given where I was in my training, Paul didn't think I needed to swim a full slate of events. But he did want me to go and swim the freestyle "mile," which was actually 1,650 yards, 66 laps in a 25-yard pool. The mile was not my event. It's not a race I swam competitively very often. I knew that, Paul knew that, and so I went into it as a sort of training swim. I broke the American record. So if I could do that—come out of nowhere and swim a record-breaking race—what's to say others couldn't also do that?

✷✷✷

We kicked off 2008 with a two-week training trip to the U.S. Olympic and Paralympic Training Center in Colorado Springs, Colorado. Eight or 10 of us from NBAC went, and Paul went as our coach. That trip, in that place, at that time, in that year, was kind of a way of saying, "All right, get ready. There's an Olympics coming."

The workouts we did there weren't all that different from the workouts we had been doing in Baltimore. The big difference was altitude. Colorado Springs is over 6,000 feet above sea level. Baltimore is less than 500 feet above sea level. When you work out at a higher altitude, you build up more red blood cells. The first few practices are rough because the air is so thin, but with time your body adapts, and once it does, you feel fine.

The Olympic Training Center is very much what its name suggests—it's a training center. You eat there. You sleep there. You stay in a dorm. You have access to anything you could possibly need to train. It's not just for swimmers—athletes in other Olympic sports train there as well. It's bare bones, and it can feel like a prison. The idea is to get you to focus and work hard, without distractions. So you eat, sleep, take care of yourself, and train. I think we went to Denver one night to go to dinner, but that was about it as far as outings went. You're so exhausted that you really don't want to do much else.

2008 was the year that Speedo introduced its new LZR Racer swimsuit, the first of the full-body swimsuits, and in doing so opened a Pandora's Box of controversy. The LZR was the brainchild of a design team which included: engineers, sports scientists, elite swimmers, and even NASA. It gave a swimmer a number of advantages, making you lighter and more buoyant, and reducing drag. Its full-body length and extreme compression squished your body, making bigger swimmers more streamlined. Critics claimed the suit gave those wearing it an unfair advantage. But all of the top swimmers wore them, which took the edge off any advantage.

There's little doubt that the LZR was effective. Between the suit's launch in February and the end of the Beijing Olympics in mid-August, 62 world records had been broken by swimmers wearing the LZR. In Beijing, LZR wearers won 94 percent of the swimming races, and they broke 23 of the 25 world records that fell. This was the most records broken at a single Olympics since 1976, when another technological innovation—swimming goggles—debuted.

In July 2009, FINA, swimming's international governing body, announced a ban of all full-body swimsuits—Speedo's and those of competitors. In the 17 months since the LZR had been introduced, more than 130 world records had fallen.

✦✦✦

The farther we got into 2008, the more people tried to make me into a female version of Michael. It made sense. We swam for the same team, we had both signed with Speedo, and we were both setting records, swimming the fastest we'd ever swum.

And as long as I was swimming the fastest I'd ever swum, the comparisons didn't bother me. I may even have welcomed them. I mean, who wouldn't want to be compared to a guy who was on his way to becoming the best and most famous swimmer ever? And although the talk about Michael possibly winning eight gold medals in Beijing started not long after the Athens Olympics, where he won six, this is swimming, a sport that really only captures the public's attention once every four years. It wasn't until the lead-up to Beijing that the media started cranking up the volume on his record. And then for me, it was like, oh, so I'm being compared to Michael? And along with that came the expectation of winning eight gold medals?

That was never realistic for me, even as well as I'd been swimming. In the best-case scenario, I had a realistic shot at winning three or four gold medals in Beijing, and I think the media would have been happy with that. I never felt that the expectation was that I had to win eight golds or be considered a failure. Besides, at the time, I was on a high. I was coming off setting a world record in 2007. In 2008, I'd broken four American records at a short course meet at the Naval Academy, and then I had that random swim where I broke the American record in the mile. It seemed like every time I got in a pool, I could produce something great. I was probably the most confident I'd ever been, though given my track record with self-confidence, you could almost predict that the other shoe was going to drop.

At the time I was dating Brennan—this was early 2008—and I remember going somewhere with him and his dad, and we were in his dad's car. I was sitting in the back seat, and Brennan and his dad were up front. Brennan's dad started asking me how I was feeling about things. He asked pretty innocent questions— he just seemed curious about what was going on in my mind at that point, a few months before the Olympic Trials. I probably told him I was feeling great, but that wasn't the most honest answer I could have given him. The truth was, everything was starting to feel real. The Olympics were about to happen. I felt excitement, sure, but also this sense of dread as the pressure and the expectations kept building. And I thought, *how in the world was I going to do this twice?* I had to get through trials, which meant swimming six events in eight days, and then I had to do it again in Beijing at the Olympics. My old frenemy, self-doubt, started creeping back in.

The general attitude of those around me seemed to be that I would come home from Beijing with a lot of gold medals. That's what was expected of me. I remember thinking, *it's not that easy, people!*

GET SET...

The first big meet of 2008 was the Missouri Grand Prix in February, at the University of Missouri in Columbia. I was coming off of training in Colorado at altitude, and I had an awesome meet, breaking the American record in the 200- and 400-freestyle and winning the 400-IM. It was a good meet for others, too, and a lot of records were broken.

Paul was very much in "let's go" mode. After I broke a 20-year-old American record in the 400-free, his approach was, "Okay, awesome job, go warm down, and get ready for the next thing." That was kind of the mentality, and I got it, but it was almost both a blessing and a curse. That was the reaction to everything I was doing at that time—awesome, cool, all right, next! There was never any stopping, never any, "Wow—you just broke an American record, and not even at a big meet. Maybe you should be excited about that!" I could be happy, but not too happy, because there was also this sense that swimming the way I was swimming was just what I was supposed to do. I was supposed to get in the pool, win races, and break records.

I realize this is all sounding a little schizophrenic. Did I have confidence, or was I riddled with self-doubt? Well both, actually, and now we're back to that idea of balance. I was still freaking out before every race and doubting whether I could win. But then I'd get in the pool and everything would change. Once I dove in I thought, *okay, I can win this. That's what I do. This is just how it's going to be.* But I would never say that out loud, outside the pool, because, you know, anything could happen. I couldn't be certain. My emotions would seesaw.

I think this uncertainty drove Paul crazy. I think he saw it as an indication that I didn't believe in myself. In fact, I did believe in myself. But how I felt about myself wasn't the only variable. Part of my doubt came from a place of respect for my competitors. On any given day, in any given race, they could pull out something crazy. My attitude was that I wanted to swim so hard that a competitor was going to have to do something spectacular to beat me.

I would obsessively stalk my competitors on the internet. Not their lives (that would be creepy), but their results. If a competitor was swimming at a meet and I wasn't there, I would pull up the meet website to keep up, hitting the refresh button on my phone over and over, more times than I care to admit. I did not want them to swim a time that beat my times. When the Australians had their Olympic Trials in March of 2008, and Stephanie Rice broke my world record in the 400-IM, I was devastated.

✶✶✶

Everything in the first half of 2008 was just prepping—working to get ready for the Olympics. I had finished high school, so there wasn't any schoolwork to do. It was literally just eat, sleep, swim, get ready for Beijing.

The focus on Beijing actually started back in 2007. That's when Visa, which was one of my sponsors, sent four of us—me, Michael, Megan Quann (now Megan Jendrick), who won two gold medals in the 2000 Olympics, and Ryan Lochte, who then was probably the best known male swimmer not named Phelps—to China for what was called the "Visa Friendship Lanes Tour," a goodwill tour to promote swimming, the Olympics, the Special Olympics (which were being held in Beijing that summer), and Visa, of course. We visited schools where we played basketball with some of the Chinese kids. We ran swimming clinics. It felt good to be giving back. You can be super selfish when you're an athlete—it's about you and your training, and it can be hard to step back from that. So when you have moments when you can give back, it feels good. When I look back, I feel incredibly fortunate to have had an opportunity like this at 17 years old.

Michael and me in China in 2007.
I will remember this trip for the rest of my life!

Our hosts took us to the Forbidden City and other sites in Beijing. They showed us visual renderings of the Water Cube, which was the architecturally striking arena where we would swim at the Olympics. The four of us pledged a contribution to the Special Olympics China of $8,808. That amount is symbolic: 8/8/08 would be the opening day of the Beijing Olympics. Michael was a celebrity at that point, with rock star status. When our van stopped, we would get swarmed by fans. We snuck in and out of pools trying not to be seen. It was just wild.

For me, I think it was in Beijing, on that tour, that it began to sink in that the whole thing was for real. That this was where we would be in a year. When you're training, it's always in the back of your mind that it's all leading up to the Olympics, but it doesn't become real until you hit the one-year mark.

✳✳✳

The closer we got to the Olympics, the more intense things got, both in and out of the pool. Each workout had a little more riding on it. Matt Lauer, from *The Today Show*, came to Meadowbrook to interview me. At times I thought I was going to pull my hair out.

To keep myself from going crazy, I signed up for a hip-hop dance class. We met every Tuesday at 7 p.m. at a studio in Towson. The teacher was a former NFL cheerleader, and she was super nice. This was me, returning to the activity I'd quit swimming for when I was five years old. We would learn different routines, and then we were supposed to perform them for the teacher at a "showcase" attended by other dancers, family and friends—an enthusiastic audience of maybe 20 people. I was so nervous. The teacher was a professional, and despite what I might have been able to do at age five, I didn't have a ton of confidence in my skills as a dancer.

It would be legitimate to ask why I—someone who focuses to an inordinate degree on anxiety, nerves, and confidence (or the lack thereof)—would sign up for a class like hip-hop, a class that had the potential to create even more nervousness and anxiety, and so many reasons to lose confidence. I think there's a good nervous and a bad nervous. If you do something that doesn't create any anxiety, then you're not going to get the same kind of endorphin hit that the right amount of anxiety can produce—the feeling that, wow! I just accomplished something challenging. I wouldn't get that endorphin hit unless something scared me a little bit.

Paul had us do some visualization exercises from time to time, but it wasn't really my thing. I tried yoga for a while, but that didn't click for me either. I'd finish yoga feeling more stressed than when I started. My mom thought things like visualization and yoga would be good for me, and God knows I had the kind of temperament where mastering a few calming techniques might have helped. But I could never slow myself down enough to the point where they did help. I can only push myself if I see a payout or a finish line—some reward I recognize as valuable. If I don't clearly see the value in something, my reaction is to say, "Well, yeah, what's the point?"

I tried Pilates for a while, and I liked it. It had purpose and value. It would strengthen my core. It would help keep me from getting injured. It just made sense.

Later, in 2009, after Beijing—I'm jumping ahead, but this is relevant—I was training with the National Team in California, and one day we went to San Diego to a Navy SEALs base, where we were going to go through a day of training like we were Navy SEALs. This meant five hours of hell. Some of the guys on the team were amped about it, but I was thinking, *how in the world is this supposed to help?* I could fall from a 60-foot rope wall, and then my season would be over. Or I could get sick from the freezing cold water (which I actually did, get sick, after they made us do up-downs in the shallow part of the freezing cold ocean, and being sick made my training suffer). We did one exercise where we had to take a raft out into the ocean and then bring it back to shore, and at one point the raft flipped up and smacked Michael in the head. He was bleeding and had to go to the doctor. They thought he might have a concussion. (It turned out he didn't.)

And my fear of falling off a wall? We had to run an obstacle course, and because it's a Navy SEAL obstacle course, you know it's going to be really hard. The SEALs test on it, and they can run it in less than 15 minutes—jumping across tires, climbing walls, all these things—but it took us about an hour. We would go through each obstacle very methodically. One of the girls in our group was going over an obstacle that was pretty high, and she fell. We weren't roped in or anything, and she just fell, and she broke her ankle. I thought, *what in the world is happening? Why in the world are we doing this?*

Granted, others may have gotten more out of this than I did; the guys in particular seemed to. Heading into it, I was already in a pretty negative place mentally and physically, feeling sore and beat up, and I had doubts about my swimming. And now I was about to do something that would make me feel worse?

I have great respect for the Navy SEALs and what they do. I think I would have gotten more out of it if we could have just sat down with them for a few hours and listened to them talk about their experiences. I could be inspired by what they do, and I could translate their experience to my own—if they can do what they do, then I can do what I do—in the pool. For me, that would have had a lot more value than spending a day trying to pretend we were Navy SEALs.

We had a sports psychologist who was working with us, and at the end of that terrible day, he said to me, "See, doesn't that make you more confident? Doesn't that make a 400-IM look like nothing?"

And I thought, *no, not even close.* Those two things are not comparable. Swimming a really hard set and hitting my paces makes a 400-IM look easier, not pretending to be a Navy SEAL for a day. I get that you need to train your mind to be strong, but the two things seemed so disconnected. If I'm training to be a Navy SEAL, then yes, I 100 percent see value in this. But for me, with swimming, what had value was doing exactly what I needed to do to prepare. And as for sports psychologists, I totally understand they can help, but shouldn't your sports psychologist be helping you with your own thoughts and feelings, and not telling you how you ought to think and feel?

I need to see the value in something in order to commit myself to it. I can only bear down on something if it makes sense to me why I'm doing it. Hitting challenging paces over and over again in a practice is something I can do. But today, go out for a run when it's cold and raining? It's very easy for me to blow it off. My husband says I'm the toughest weakest person he's ever known.

So, getting back to the hip-hop classes—they were fun. At our showcase we danced to "Here I Come," by Fergie. The value of the class was to take my mind off of my swimming, to help me feel normal, and at a time when the pressure was mounting—when the music in my head was getting turned up louder and louder because the Olympics were getting closer and closer.

Watch my interview with *The Today Show*.

"HOFF THE CHARTS!"

The 2008 Olympic Trials were held at the Qwest Center (now called the CenturyLink Center) in Omaha, Nebraska, in late June and early July. I entered six events: the 100-, 200-, 400-, and 800-freestyle, and the 200- and 400-IM. I went in feeling very confident, almost like the calm before the storm.

Trials started on June 29, and we arrived three or four days early to settle into our hotel rooms and get acclimated. You can ask any swimmer—those are the worst, *worst* days. You just want the meet to get started. You're tired of thinking about it. I spent too much time overanalyzing everything as it was, and now I had an extra three days to do that? It's like, how do I feel? How do my legs feel when I walk up a flight of steps? How tired are they? I felt confident, but—me being me—I remember also feeling this tiny tug of anxiousness.

First the calm, then the storm—literally. Two nights before trials started there was a tornado warning, and we had to leave our hotel rooms and go down into the basement. We sat there for about an hour. I'm an East Coast girl, and my knowledge of tornadoes is limited to what I know from watching the movie Twister, but if you live in Nebraska, I don't think you'd consider what we experienced to be a really big deal. Though it may have been a kind of metaphor—for what, I wasn't sure.

When they let us go back to our rooms, we had to use the stairs, six flights' worth, and I remember thinking, *don't go too fast because you need to be sure your legs are relaxed and ready for your races.* Here we're coming out of a tornado warning, and I was thinking of everything possible that could wreck trials for me. These were not entirely rational thoughts.

The 400-IM prelims and finals were on the first day of trials. I was so nervous. The way my meets started set the tone for how my whole meet was going to go—it wasn't like me to have a terrible race to start out and then turn around and have an awesome race afterward. So my first event was extremely important. And there was added pressure on this race. I'd set the world record in the 400-IM in 2007, but Stephanie Rice, from Australia, had broken it in March at the Australian Olympic Trials. I would have liked nothing more than to win it back.

I won it back, with a time of 4:31.12, finishing more than a second and a half ahead of Elizabeth Beisel, who came in second. It was maybe the best race of my life.

There were more than 12,000 people in the Qwest Center, and it could get loud inside, especially in the middle of a race when people realized they were about to see a world record get broken. The cheering definitely hypes you up, especially if you're ahead, and especially in strokes like breaststroke where you can actually hear it. For the other strokes it's more like background noise. You mostly just hear water. It's great to know the crowd is there and cheering for you, and maybe there's a little adrenaline bump, but the truth is, at that point I'm so focused on what I'm doing that the crowd isn't a major factor. Some swimmers are great at acknowledging the crowd, playing to the crowd, connecting with the crowd. I'm not one of them. There's this moment before a big race where the announcer introduces you, and usually you smile and do a little wave to the crowd. I always hated that part. I hated smiling and waving. I was locked in; in a zone, blocking everything out, and I didn't want to do anything that could interfere with that. I get that when there are people cheering for you—you want to acknowledge that, but I just felt like I was being so fake.

It understates things to say it's a big thrill to set a world record, and if you watch the video of that event, and see my reaction, my sort of signature mouth-wide-open look, you can tell I'm thrilled. I'm thinking, *thank God. This means I'm ready. This means I'm in condition. And this means trials are going to go well because of how I just swam.*

Kicking off trials with a world record take back!

My whole family was there—they were about 15 rows deep, up in the stands, and they held a sign that read, "Hoff the Charts!" So it felt awesome to be able to do that with them there.

*I felt so lucky to have so many family members cheering me on.
Looking up and seeing this sign was awesome.*

But afterward, I didn't even get to eat dinner with them. They had a dinner set up in the Qwest Center for swimmers, and after that I was able to meet my parents at my hotel for only 15 or 20 minutes. It was about 9 p.m., and I had to get up early in the morning for my next race.

I never get emotional in public—at least not for happy stuff. But that night, lying in bed in my hotel room in Omaha, I got choked up. More than happiness, what I felt was relief—relief that I'd won the race, relief that I'd won back the world record, relief that the meet was off to a good start. Relief from proving that I could do what I came to do. I thought, *this is good. This is going to go well.*

Beisel (no one who knows her well calls her "Elizabeth") was 15, swimming in her first trials, and by coming in second, she ended up being the youngest swimmer to make the U.S. Olympic swim team. I was happy for her, and I could relate to what she'd just experienced. We had a big hug after the race.

The 400-freestyle was the next day, and it went well—not as well as the 400-IM had gone, but pretty darned well. Halfway through the race I was in fourth place, so I had to crank it up a bit in the second half of the race. In the water I had a kind of confidence that I could do whatever I needed to do to overcome adversity. So I didn't panic—I just trusted that my training would kick in, and I could climb back in front. I didn't swim my best time, but I was close to my best time, and I won the race, so that meant I'd made the Olympic team in a second event. Two days, two races, two wins, two events on the Olympic team. Check, check.

That's kind of how it felt, like the trials would last for eight days, and each day had a box next to it, and it was my job to check that box and then move on to the next one. Everything felt set up so that winning the races was what I was supposed to do. Okay, sure, when I broke the world record in the 400-IM I got pretty pumped. But in terms of just winning the races and making the team, that was just what I was supposed to do.

Of course, doing it is easier said than done. Every single race was so different. My strokes were feeling really connected to the water and powerful so that gave me a really solid foundation and a lot of confidence. But in every race, I faced different people and there were different circumstances. On day two, I had the 400-free, and on day three, I would have to swim four races—the prelims and semifinals for both the 200-free and the 200-IM, with the finals in both events on day four. And I would be swimming against really intense competition, so the box for each day wasn't one I could just automatically check off. I didn't feel at all like I had those races in the bag. I was competing against really good swimmers who wanted to win and wanted to make the Olympic team every bit as much as I did. I wasn't a robot. I was a person. I was fallible. These things stressed me out.

Paul had this look—this look that I would call his "intense eyes," a look that was almost aggressive, and I would tell him that look would stress me out. So before the 200-free and the 200-IM, he agreed he wasn't going to give me the intense eyes look. I needed to be calm at that point; he understood that. I needed to trust my training and turn off my mind. Things right then could have gone one way, or they could have gone the other. With two races and two wins under my belt, part of me was feeling confident, but part of me was worrying that I wasn't going to be able to pull all of this off. Because you don't pull anything off until you actually pull it off, and I'd never swum a schedule as intense and packed as what I swam at trials. Swimmers swim two, or three, or four events in a session all the time, and I'd done that many times before, but never at an Olympic Trials where I swam against some of the best swimmers in the nation—trying to win races back to back, 35 minutes apart. But I'd done the preparation. Now I just had to swim the races.

I won the 200-free in a really close race, beating Allison Schmitt by four hundredths of a second, and both of us were less than a second ahead of Julia Smit, in third. And I won the 200-IM, coming in ahead of Natalie Coughlin in second and Ariana Kukors in third. I set American records in both races. The races were back to back, and I remember leaving the pool after the 200-IM and running to the award stand to get my medal for the 200-free, brushing my hair as I went. This was a challenging double, and I felt great pride and relief at having just pulled it off.

By the end of day four, I had swum four 400s (prelims and finals in the 400-free and the 400-IM) and six 200s (prelims, semifinals, and finals in the 200-free and 200-IM). And I'd won all four of the events I'd entered. I kept checking the boxes. Four days, four wins—check, check, check, check.

The schedule at trials was the same schedule we would have for the Olympics, so in the midst of all this, way back in the back of my mind, I was aware that I'd have to do this all over again in a little over a month in Beijing. Only there it would be harder, because I'd be swimming not just against the best American swimmers, but against the best in the world.

Day five was the prelims and semifinals in the 100-freestyle. I did okay in my prelim, but when I got to the semifinals, I just didn't have much pop. I just didn't swim a good race, and I didn't qualify for the finals. This and the 50-free were races for the sprinter girls, and I didn't feel like I belonged with them. I was a versatile athlete, but I was never a super powerful athlete. I'm more of a mid-distance swimmer, and my versatility leans more toward the endurance side of things, so those shorter races are outside my sweet spot. I wasn't too disappointed. Not advancing was kind of a blessing in disguise, because it meant that my only race on day six would be the prelims of the 800-freestyle.

I remember waking up on day six and getting ready to go to the Qwest Center, and on my way out I saw a headline making a big deal out of the fact that I hadn't advanced in the 100-free. I thought, *are you kidding me? I won four events and the media was going to focus on the one race so far that I hadn't won?* I didn't think it was worth a headline.

I felt pretty good going into the 800-free prelims. I was never going to just cruise in a race, but I wanted to use the prelims to feel out the competition and see if I could make it to the final without exerting 100 percent effort. Qualifying for finals is based on time, but if you finish in the top two in your prelim heat, you're a pretty safe bet to make it to the finals. And the race is over eight minutes long, so that gives you time to adjust.

If you find you're not where you want to be at 400 meters, you can ramp things up a little.

I went into the finals of the 800-free with the second fastest qualifying time, behind Kate Zeigler. Kate was an outstanding distance swimmer. In 2007, she broke Janet Evans' world record in the 1,500-freestyle, a record that had stood for nearly 20 years, and Kate held that record for six more years, until Katie Ledecky broke it in 2013. The media loved the whole "Kate vs. Katie" thing. We weren't enemies. And later we'd become friends. Let's say that in 2008 we were cordial. But there was definitely this "Kate vs. Katie" energy that the media created that made us rivals.

Before the race, I went to the wrong lane. I went to lane four, which is where the swimmer with the top qualifying time gets placed. In the 800-free, that was Kate, not me. I didn't do this to be arrogant—I was just so focused that I wasn't thinking about what I was doing. She tapped me on the shoulder and said, "Um, I think you're supposed to be over there." She pointed to lane five. It was so embarrassing.

I won the race. Kate came in second. My Olympic Trials were done, and a great sense of relief washed over me. I qualified in five events and won all of them. At the time I don't think I had a real appreciation for what I'd just done. It made complete sense, at that point, for the media to compare me to Michael Phelps. We had both just won five events at the Olympic Trials. He'd set two world records, and I'd set one. To this day, that was the best meet of my life!

2008 200 IM AR.   2008 200 free AR.

But finishing the Olympic Trials meant I was in the vortex. So I had to say goodbye to my family for six weeks and say goodbye to my boyfriend. We were headed to training camp, and after that, to Beijing.

A tornado, of course, is a big, swirling vortex. Maybe I'd found my metaphor.

SPECTATORS

I have a love/hate relationship with spectators. On one hand, when I'm winning, they lift me up, make me feel special, like a rock star, even. Hearing 14,000 people roar when I touch the wall brings on an almost indescribable feeling. On the other hand, failing in front of these people leaves me feeling humiliated and full of shame. Too many spectators like to react in ways that reinforce those feelings. Social media has only made things worse.

When I watch sports, I feel deeply for the athletes who lose or make mistakes. I hate it when the cameras zoom in on faces full of pain. I know what that feels like to be that person with the camera in their face, and it breaks my heart to watch. I will rush to the defense of people who screw up, especially if they're young and it's clear they're giving their best. It's like, what gives you the right to slam some 19-year-old wide receiver for dropping a pass?

TRAINING CAMP

Just like in 2004, after trials we flew to Palo Alto for a couple of weeks of training at Stanford. I was much better prepared than I had been four years earlier. When I went to Omaha for trials, I didn't know how many events I would qualify for in Beijing, but I was pretty confident that I was going to make the team. So I prepared for that. I had my suitcase packed. I was ready. The reality of going away for six weeks didn't catch me by surprise this time. After trials I think we stayed maybe one more day in Omaha and then flew to California.

Training camp at Stanford went well. We had beautiful weather, and a great hotel. I was roommates with the person I wanted to room with—Kathleen Hersey, who qualified in the 200-butterfly—so everything felt very comfortable. And the training camp at Stanford was still far enough out from the actual Olympics that things felt fresh. I could feel a little bit of a monkey on my back, but I wasn't close to the point where that monkey could make me panic.

We had our assignments each day at practice, and we trained. I ended up being more involved this time around in our media day when the reporters came in to chat with our team and *Sports Illustrated* came to do a photo shoot, but most of the time, when we weren't practicing, we'd just hang out or go to the mall. We'd watch TV. We played a lot of Risk—anything to distract ourselves from what was happening next.

✳✳✳

At Stanford in 2004, I felt like the little kid. Back then there were at least two swimmers on the team who didn't exactly go out of their way to make me feel otherwise. I wasn't too disappointed they weren't on the team in 2008. This time around a group of us grew pretty close—Kathleen, Caroline Burkle, Allison Schmitt, and me. And unlike 2004, I felt pretty comfortable with just about everyone on the team. Natalie Coughlin, Dara Torres, and Amanda Beard were named as captains, and they helped set a positive tone. I felt a lot of support from Amanda in particular. She had been 14 in 1996 when she made her first Olympic team, so the experience of being the young kid at the Olympics was something we had in common. I got along well with the others, too. It was maybe the first time I'd been with a group of girls where we were all on the same level, and we all understood what we were going through. We could just hang out and be girls. So that part was pretty cool.

Elizabeth Beisel was 15 years old and in her first Olympics. She's talked about how isolating swimming could be for her as a young teenager. In Beijing, I let her know that if she needed anything, to please tell me. I told her I'd been where she was and I understood what it was like and what she might be going through. We weren't close friends then—that came later. I was four years older than she was, and we moved in different orbits. I just wanted her to know that I had her back.

Leadership on the men's side was pretty awesome, too. Erik Vendt, Jason Lezak, and Brendan Hansen were selected as captains. Those guys are great guys, and they would make it fun.

I get asked a lot about my relationship with Michael. Michael and I were friends. He teased me and, most of the time, he'd get a rise out of me, but it was all in fun. I remember once, he filled my mesh bag that I took with me to practice with orange peels. He would do stuff like that. That was just his personality. "Katie is like a younger sister I never had," Michael told the Baltimore Sun in 2007, after I broke the world record in the 400-IM. "She is such a trooper, it's unreal. She takes so much grief from all of us…It's fun."

Paul was now an official Olympic coach, so he was with us all the time. The thing with Michael and the orange peels? Paul was definitely not thrilled about it. He worried that things like that would distract me, which was pretty much the point.

✶✶✶

After Stanford, we flew to Singapore to train and adjust to the time difference. All the moving around is one of the hardest parts about all of this. People were saying, "Okay, we're going to change your whole environment—your teammates, the other people around you, the city you're in, your coach, maybe—but in the pool we want you to replicate your best performances." I'm a creature of habit, so that's always an adjustment. It takes time for new habits to form.

I missed Brennan. He had become my grounding point. Back in Baltimore, we could have a hard training day, and then we'd go back to my house where we'd just chill out and watch *The Office*. He could help me focus on something other than swimming. More importantly, he was my support system. We said goodbye in Omaha, so we'd been apart since then, but I missed him even more when we left California for Singapore. We'd talk on Skype, and that helped, but it wasn't the same.

Brennan was pretty incredible by the amount of support he showed me. When I flipped in fourth place halfway through the 400-freestyle at the trials in Omaha, he was up in the stands stressing out trying to figure out what he would say to console me in case I lost. When I was in Beijing, and he was back in

Baltimore, he'd stay up until the early hours of the morning so he could call me after races. He truly went above and beyond, especially considering his age. This poor kid was 17 years old and he had to bear that kind of stress just to date me. What other high school boyfriend does that?

★★★

We flew to Singapore on Singapore Airlines, and that was awesome. It was a 17-hour flight, and most of us were in business class, but if you held some kind of record you got seated in first class. First class was ridiculous. Your seat had a door. You ate on fine china. You had a full bed. Take away what we were flying to Singapore to do, and I might have been able to enjoy this properly. It was a reminder of how crazy everything was right then. To this day, that was the best flight I've ever had.

Training camp was a very controlled environment, but came with a lot of positive features. Our hotel was gorgeous. They set out a buffet prestigious enough for royalty. You could even get spa treatments. The pool where we practiced was spectacular. We saw monkeys, and it felt like paradise. Like with the flight, I wish I'd been in a place in my head where I could have appreciated Singapore more. I didn't want to go out into the city. I didn't want to go to spas. I just felt like time was ticking, and I needed to stay focused on Beijing.

Paul and I had a fight during training. I can't remember the specifics. He wanted me to do one thing, and I told him I didn't think I wanted to do it that way, and things went downhill from there. In my "Katie-focused haze," I may not have fully understood this at the time, but these Olympics must have been hard for him, too. These were his first Games as an official coach. He was young for a coach—in his early 30s—and even though he was among coaches with a ton of Olympic experience, I'm not sure he really sought them out for advice or guidance. As for me, I was happy to spend what spare time I had hanging out with teammates. When I went to dinner, who was I going to go with—people like Caroline and Kathleen, or with Paul and Sean (Hutchison, another coach), so we could talk about sets and intervals and times and medals? It wasn't a hard decision. I feel certain that the amount of time I spent with Paul was less than what he wanted. But again, I was looking to him to be my coach, not my best friend.

Heading into Singapore, I was happy with my training. I'd been swimming well. The trials had been a big success. But the pressure was still there, a lot of it self-imposed. Every workout had to be a strong workout, because I needed the confidence that came from swimming well in training. One person I especially enjoyed working out with was Kara Lynn Joyce, a sprinter who'd made the team in the 50-freestyle. We'd go head to head on pull sets (sets we'd swim with a pull buoy), and we'd pump out some crazy times. I was happy with the times I was swimming, but it was all very stressful. With every practice, I'd think, *Okay, here's a measure of where I am. Here's a measure of how it's going to go in Beijing.*

Our training didn't change a lot. We had tapered some before trials, so now we had to ramp things back up, and this meant swimming some 6,000- or 7,000-meter workouts, so there were definitely some hard days. Sometimes I'd swim workouts with the group, and sometimes I'd swim them solo. As we got closer to the start of the Games, I think I may have isolated myself a little bit. As is my pattern, I was a jumbled mix of confidence blended with stress and nerves, and the closer we got to August 8, stress and nerves made up a bigger part of that mix. It felt like there was a barbell on my shoulders, with more five-pound and ten-pound weights added every day. I told myself, *It's fine. You're fine. It's all good.* But still, a part of me thought, *am I going to be able to do this?*

After about a week and a half of training in Singapore, we flew to Beijing. When we landed, the sky was orange from all the pollution. I remember texting my parents, a few friends, and

Brennan and telling them that. After I sent the text my phone just shut down for about five minutes. I thought, *oh, wow. Somebody doesn't like me sending texts about the orange sky. We really are in China. This is for real.*

THE THRILL OF VICTORY, THE AGONY OF DEFEAT

Everything else melts away and you're left with a feeling of pure happiness—happiness that comes from knowing you just put all of yourself into something and accomplished something extraordinary. I think there are distinctions between victory and winning. Lots of people win. Fewer achieve true victory. True victory carries weight because it's rare. And true victory is fleeting, because once you achieve it, you recalibrate expectations, reset the bar, and start pursuing it all over again.

Defeat, on the other hand, is a break with reality because everything you worked so hard for has just slipped through your fingers. It radiates throughout your body and your mind, accompanied, for me, by shame, embarrassment, and pain.

I think about defeat to the point of unhealthy obsession. The rational me should look for the positive in defeat, should look for what's to be learned from losing. But in the moment of defeat, the rational me has vanished. I wonder how long the pain will last. I wish I could be someone else.

Defeat feels agonizing because I care, a lot, and if I didn't, I wouldn't be me. I wouldn't be the person who puts everything on the line, who takes the risk, who accepts the vulnerability that comes with the possibility of losing. And it's that risk, that vulnerability, that makes victory, when it comes, so sweet.

GO!

(BEIJING)

August 8, 2008. That was the date of the start of the XXIX Summer Olympics in Beijing. The numerals 08/08/08 made a triply lucky date in China, where eight is a lucky number, signifying wealth, or prosperity, or good fortune, or all three. I've heard that some Chinese women try to plan their pregnancies so their babies would be born on that day. The opening ceremonies began at eight minutes and eight seconds after 8 p.m.—at 08:08:08 on 08/08/08, in other words—just to pile more luck on top of luck.

We arrived in Beijing maybe four days earlier, so August 4. Four is not a lucky number in China. In fact, it's a very unlucky number, associated with death. Houses that have a four in their address sell for less than houses without. I may be superstitious about my training routines—when to warm up, when to stretch, those kinds of things—but thankfully I'm not about Chinese numbers, or this might have felt like an omen. Maybe we arrived on August 5. It's hard to remember.

We took a shuttle from the airport to the Olympic Village, and then went through the whole process of checking in, filling out paperwork, getting our credentials, and so on. And then we were in. You wear your credentials on a lanyard around your neck—they're what you use to get into the Village, to get meals at the cafeteria—were your official ID for the Games. Security is tight, and only athletes and official Olympic coaches and trainers can come and go as they please. The Olympic Village literally is like a little village, with a cafeteria, a post office, a barbershop and gift shops. And the dorms were not the most glamorous part of the Games. Some people did a lot of exploring in the Village, but I did almost none until all of my events were over. For me, it was pool, food, dorm, repeat.

Being an Olympian, representing my country, was an enormous honor. But the whole thing felt very surreal. I thought, *this is it. This is what I've been preparing for the last four years.*

★★★

We trained in two pools. One was the Water Cube, the racing venue, with its space age design and blue bubble exterior. It was about a 20-minute shuttle ride from the Village. The other was a training pool in the Village. Finals for races were in the morning, so the Village pool was very convenient on days when I wanted to get up early and get in a swim to warm up my body before a race.

It's hard to remember the specifics of our workouts before the races started, but basically at this point we were trying to stay sharp but conserve energy, to save it for the races. I might do 50 meters of butterfly off the blocks just to get used to the feel of it. Or I'd do 50 meters where I'd want to hit the pace I wanted to swim in a 400-meter race, and I wanted to hit that pace without feeling like I had to work really hard to get there. With the races looming, there was a lot of pressure, and constant analysis. This was the worst time. The day-to-day was mundane. I felt like I should have been having fun. I mean, I was an Olympian! I was at the Olympic Games! But I just wanted the races to hurry up and start.

I tried hard to stay calm, because I could feel the pressure start to mount. It was how I felt before the Olympic Trials, only ratcheted up about five notches from that. People tried to calm me down by saying things like, "Oh, you know, the Olympics is just a meet like any other." Well, no. The Olympics is not just a meet like any other. It's the Olympics, the one time in four years where the whole world suddenly cares about swimming. There's an entirely different feel and buzz in the air, with tension hanging over everything. Everyone's trying to put on this air of calm, but no one is actually calm. We'd have media sessions where we'd talk to the press, and I'd tell them I was so excited— that it was such an honor to be on Team USA, and I was really looking forward to racing. There's a part of me that thought, *well, why don't we just put it out there that we're nervous and freaking out, instead of all this pretending that we're not?* It took more effort to pretend. At least that was my perspective. I might have felt differently if I was just swimming maybe one "shortish" race and then maybe a couple of relays. But with prelims and finals, I was going to have to attack four 400s and six 200s all in the first four days.

It wasn't just the athletes—the coaches were feeling the pressure, too. It had to be hard for them. It's their job to see to it that we do well, but once the race starts, they're basically helpless. So in the days leading up to the races, they're all about positive energy. They would go around asking, "Are you good? Are you good?"

And I'd say, "Yeah, I'm good."

"Are you excited?"

"Yeah, I'm excited! Ready to go!" It was on a repeat reel. But inside I was thinking, *can we just get to the races?*

With this being Paul's first time as an official Olympic coach, it had to be hard for him. We worked together at the pool, but we didn't talk a lot outside of that. In the days leading up to the first race, I didn't feel comfortable talking to him about how I was feeling, how everything that was headed my way felt like... like a lot. That's not a conversation I would have with anybody else either. Acknowledging how I felt deep down would communicate that I wasn't prepared. And my moods would fluctuate. Sometimes I'd say, "I'm good! I feel great! I'm good to go!" And I'd really mean it. And then at other times I'd wonder where that thing came from that kept gnawing at me. *All these events—how am I going to get through this?* At those times I didn't enjoy being an Olympian. I just wanted it to go well and then be done.

✳✳✳

I skipped the opening ceremonies, the parade of athletes, all of that. Swimming events are held during the first week of the Games, so if you're a swimmer, unless you don't swim until later in the week, there's a good chance you'll skip the opening festivities.

The prelims for the 400 individual medley were in the evening of Day 2, August 9. I won my prelim, and I put in a really solid swim. I felt relief—not huge relief, but more like, *okay, that's done, check the box.* It doesn't matter if it's a state championship or the Olympics, every swimmer will tell you this—getting that first swim out of the way means a lot. It's a way of telling yourself, *all right, we're underway.*

After you finish your race, it's not like you just walk out of the building and go back to your dorm. You warm down. You get a massage. Eventually you get dressed and get back on the bus. That night it was 10 or 10:30 p.m. by the time I got back to the Village, ate something, and made it back to my dorm room. As nervous as I was, I never had a problem with eating. I could eat what I wanted, sometimes up to 30 minutes or so before a race, and it wouldn't bother me. And as terrible as I was at turning my mind off during the day, it wasn't the same with sleeping. Some people might lie awake all night staring at the ceiling, but I was a good sleeper. That night I still had time for seven or so hours of sleep before I got up at 6 a.m. the next morning to do a warmup swim.

***

When we got to the Water Cube Sunday morning, it was eerily quiet. The only swimmers there were the ones who had a semifinal or a final that morning. Jon Urbanchek, one of our coaches, was there cracking jokes, trying to keep things light. There's just a different vibe for a final.

Before races, I had a routine. An hour and a half before the race, I'd do my first warmup. Then I'd stretch, and maybe 30 minutes before the race I'd do my second warmup. In Beijing, there were plenty of warmup pools, so finding a place to do this was never a problem. After my second warmup, I'd get a shake-down from the massage people, to keep my muscles loose, and then I'd report to the ready room 15 or 20 minutes before the race. I felt really good before the race. I still had some nerves, but nothing out of the ordinary. I wasn't ranked first, but I had a very smooth prelim, and I was confident I could get back to my best times.

Elizabeth Beisel swam the best time in prelims, so she was in lane four. I was in lane five, between Beisel and Stephanie Rice, from Australia, in lane six. Stephanie and I had traded the world record back and forth a couple of times already that year. She took it from me at the Australian Olympic Trials in March, and I took it back from her at the U.S. trials just five weeks earlier. So I would be swimming with a lot of very strong swimmers. I was confident, but I wasn't thinking, *Oh, I've got this.*

Control what you can control. That's what I was thinking.

The media likes intense rivalries, but the fact was, out of the pool Stephanie and I got along just fine. We weren't best friends at that time, but it wasn't like we hated each other either. It was the same with Kirsty Coventry, a South African swimmer who was in lane one. I'd been racing her since 2004, and we were also friendly out of the pool. You get to know your competitors.

Earlier that morning Michael had won the men's 400-IM—his first gold medal in Beijing—and before our race he came by and tapped Beisel and me on the head, saying, "Let's go, guys." I remember thinking, *God I wish I was him, and had already finished the race, and won gold.* There's that moment before you get paraded out to the starting blocks. It reminds me of being on a roller coaster, where you start that slow climb before the plunge—click, click, click, up, up, up. That's what it feels like. I hate roller coasters.

When I watch swimming now on TV, I think about that moment when all the swimmers parade out in their warmups to the starting blocks, and it looks pretty cool. The crowd roars, you wave and smile—it looks like fun. I wish I had learned to enjoy it more in the moment. I always sped through, throwing my Ugg boots and sweats into my basket as fast as I could so I could put goggles on and get ready to race. I hated feeling rushed.

I swam the first half of the race—butterfly and backstroke—at about the same time I had swum at the Olympic Trials in Omaha, maybe even a little faster. But halfway through the race—after those two strokes—I was way behind. Later Paul would criticize me for not attacking the first half of the race more. But in the race, I doubted that would be a smart thing to do, because breaststroke comes next, and it's my strongest stroke, and if I attacked harder in the first 200 meters, I'd be out of gas for the breaststroke.

Breaststroke went okay, but not great. Maybe I wasn't relaxed enough, or just didn't have as much pop, but my split was nearly a second slower than I had swum at trials. By the time we got to the last 100 meters—freestyle—I was feeling kind of helpless. I could see Kirsty ahead of me over in lane one, and I could see the splashes of Stephanie's feet out in front of me in lane six, so I was pretty sure I wasn't going to win. I just wanted to finish strong. At this point I was in this battle and just kept fighting. I was in third. I wasn't going to win gold. In the midst of the race, there's less emotion there than you would think—you just swim.

Going into the race, I knew Stephanie would be tough to beat, but could I have guessed she was going to become the first woman in the world to swim under four minutes and 30 seconds, and drop another two seconds off the world record? Or that Kirsty, in second place, would be the second woman to go under 4:30? No. I had no idea that was going to happen. So hats off to them; both of them swam a great race.

As for me, I came in third, and I was definitely disappointed. I took some consolation in the fact that I had a pretty solid swim, only about a half second off my world record from trials. At trials I was freaking out and so happy. Now it was Steph's turn to freak out and be happy. Watching that from the next lane over wasn't easy. I'd won my first Olympic medal, bronze, not gold, but still. I'd ripped off the Band-Aid and handled the pressure pretty well. I still had five more events to swim.

My first Olympic medal race!

But I was bummed because the 400-IM was always a point of pride for me. I'd held the world record, and in my mind that race was my best shot at a gold medal. After the race, the media looked at me like, *Are you happy with bronze? Should we be happy for you?* Watch the video of the medal ceremony—I don't look happy. You could be the 10th seed and finish third and be thrilled. When you're a favorite to win the race, and finish third, you're not thrilled. I came in with the world record, and I left with a bronze medal.

I had six hours before I'd be back up on the blocks for the prelims of the 400-free. I figured that meant I could go back to the Olympic Village, decompress for a few minutes, eat, maybe take a quick nap, go to a team meeting, and then get back on the bus to go back to the Water Cube for my next race. But things didn't work out the way I'd envisioned.

Something was bugging Paul. We were on the bus back to the Village, and I was texting my parents. I tried to talk on the phone with Brennan as well. But I looked at Paul, in the sunglasses he always wore, and I could tell something was off. By this point I'd known him for years, so I could tell when something's going on with him. When we got off the bus, I asked him what was up. He shrugged it off, "Oh, nothing." He suggested we go get something to eat. When we finished and were walking out of the cafeteria, I pushed it. "What is going on?"

We walked to a seating area just behind the dorms. That's when he let it rip. He told me that I wasn't really going after the gold. That I didn't attack the race the way I should have. That I wasn't doing everything in my power to win.

This was the ultimate insult. To this day, when someone accuses me of not doing everything I can at something, of not having the integrity to try my hardest, it's a trigger. I always give it my all. When he said that, I remember thinking, *I have 4,000 meters of racing left to do. How are you bringing this up right now? We just spent four years building toward these games, and now that I need you the most, instead of trying to build me up, you're tearing me down?*

In that moment, I knew that it wasn't going to work for him to continue as my coach in the future.

I went back to my dorm room and cried and cried. I just bawled my eyes out. At some point I had to go to our women's team meeting, and before I left, I put extra eyeliner on, way thicker than normal, so no one could see how puffy my eyes were. Then it was back to the pool for the prelims of the 400-freestyle, where I had to make sure I finished in the top eight.

✳✳✳

Back at the Water Cube, my face layered with eyeliner so no one could see I'd been crying, I watched the 400-freestyle prelims that came before mine. Everyone was taking it out so fast. I'd see what their times were like at the halfway mark, and I thought, *dear God, this is going to be a fast race*. My prelim went okay, though. I think I went into the final with the third fastest time.

The 400-free was a weird race for me. I wanted badly to win gold, but I had never won an international medal in the 400-free. It could be anyone's race, and because I wasn't the favorite I didn't feel as much pressure. I was still nervous, but not in the same way.

The prelims with all of the fast starts stayed in my head as I got ready for the final the next morning. Paul and I talked strategy. The idea was for me to hang as close as I could to whoever was leading, and then reel them in over the last 200 meters. Paul was really positive, but it felt to me like he was trying too hard, like he was trying to overcompensate for his negative outburst after the 400-IM. I had not forgotten how he'd torn into me after that race, nor had I forgiven him, but I'm good at compartmentalizing, I put that earlier conversation to the side and tried to stay focused on the race in front of me.

In the finals, everything was different. After the fast starts in the prelims, everyone started out super slow. I don't think I took it out too fast, but after 200 meters, I was ahead by a significant amount, which was confusing. I decided to run with it. In the world of perfect hindsight, I might have done things differently, might have eased off a little bit, but in the moment I pushed the pedal down hard through 350 meters, and even though I had a substantial lead at the last turn, I had nothing left. Over the last length of the pool, my lead got smaller and smaller. In the last 25 meters I just bore down and did everything I could to get to the wall. I swam in lane three, and Rebecca Adlington was two lanes over in five, closing the gap. We reached out for the wall and touched. I came up out of the water and listened for the announcer, thinking, *please, let me hear my name.* But he said, "Rebecca Adlington," and I looked at the scoreboard to confirm it. In less time than it takes to blink your eyes, she touched first and won gold, and I touched seven hundredths of a second after her and got silver.

Seven hundredths of a second. That's what separates Katie Hoff, Olympic medalist from Katie Hoff, Olympic champion. At the time, I had no idea how significant those seven hundredths of a second would be. If I had won the 400-IM the day before—I was favored to, after all—coming in second by seven hundredths of a second in this race would have been a little less painful. Even in the moment, it wasn't all that big of a deal. I felt more pride than discouragement. I had four races left. Surely I'd win a gold medal in at least one of them. But that didn't happen. Seven hundredths of a second was the closest I would get to gold. And as time passed—days, months, years—being that close just got more and more painful.

People have told me that I lifted my head up at the finish. Not a lot—just a little. I don't know. Did that make the difference? If I'd kept my head down, would I be an Olympic gold medalist? Who knows? There are so many ifs. If I'd just swum my best time, I would have won gold. If I hadn't pushed so hard in the first 300 meters, I would have won gold. If I'd gone in with a better race strategy, I would have won gold. To this day, it's the race I play back in my mind and obsess over. It's the race where I keep going back and saying, "If I'd only done X, or Y, or Z."

✳✳✳

Everything in Beijing just felt hard. I didn't feel like I had the same kind of easy speed that I had at the Olympic Trials five weeks earlier. And I remember being very aware of how much more taxing the schedule was than at trials. The swimming schedule may have been identical, but there was all the blood testing, and the press conferences, and the shuttling back and forth to the Olympic Village. All of this on top of nearly 5,000 meters' worth of races between the heats and the finals, and the competition was so stiff that in Beijing I couldn't pace the prelims or a semifinal the way I liked to have. I had to go all out or nearly all out every time. And that's what I ended up trying to do, which was just too much for how many events I swam. I felt exhausted mentally and emotionally and physically. I tried to stay focused on navigating through each race, but after two days, with five more still to come, I was very aware that I still had a lot of boxes left to check.

✳✳✳

In the evening after the 400-free, we had the prelims for both the 200-freestyle and the 200-IM. I was upset—about my races so far, about my blowup with Paul after the 400-IM—but I didn't have any time to sit around feeling sorry for myself. There just wasn't any time to dwell on it. I had to go back to the Village, get a massage, get a shakeout, eat, take a nap, go to the team meeting, then go back to the pool for two more races. I had to just push forward. It was like a mantra running through my head—*This is what I do. This is what I have to do.*

In the 200-meter races, I swam a preliminary heat and then a semifinal before the final race, so my goal for Monday evening was to swim a solid race and finish in the top 16 in both. I was on autopilot and I qualified easily. I knew what I could do and tried to conserve some energy by swimming at slightly less than 100 percent effort. Maybe 95 percent. It's a balancing act, but with four events still to go, I didn't want to leave it all in the pool in a preliminary heat. I made the semifinals easily in both races.

In the semifinals the next morning, I cranked it back up to 100 percent. I aimed for top two in my heat. There were two semifinal races, and the top eight swimmers with the best times advanced. Finishing in the top three usually got you through to the finals, but it's risking things a little. Top two is much safer. This also went well, and I qualified for the finals in both races.

The finals for the 200-freestyle and the 200-IM were the next day, Wednesday. The 200-free came first. Through the whole race, I thought I was going so slow. I thought I was thrashing, and everything felt hard. It wasn't until afterward, when I spoke to a reporter, that I realized I'd swum the fastest 200-free I'd ever swum, and I set a new American record. That was the good news. The not so good news was that I finished fourth. Frederica Pellegrini, from Italy, won the race, and broke her own world record doing so. Sara Isakovic from Slovenia took silver. To this day she has Slovenia's only Olympic medal for swimming. Jiaying Pang from China took the bronze. Normally when I set an American record I was elated. I wasn't elated. But I didn't have time to get too disappointed. I had to get ready for the 200-IM.

So much of how I felt about myself depended on my perspective. A month and a half before, at the Olympic Trials, I had also broken the American record in the 200-free. But I had won the race, and that left me riding high going into the 200-IM. I was tired, but it was a lot easier to keep that positive energy going and fight through fatigue when I had just finished first rather than it is when I finished fourth. In Beijing, it was like every swim I had poured water into a glass—in a bad way. Every race added a little more of the bad water. And at that point, three races in, I felt like the water in the glass was getting awfully close to the top.

The 200-IM was so painful. I took out the first 100 meters— butterfly and backstroke—way too hard, and that meant I didn't have what I needed for the breaststroke, which is normally my best weapon. I felt like I was carrying 20 pounds of sandbags—I was sinking, I had no forward movement, and I kind of died in the last 50 meters. I finished fourth again—it was not a good swim for me.

After the race, the media devoured again: "Do you think this was too much? Do you think you should have done all of this? Do you think you're swimming too many races?" It just added more bad water to the glass. When I was winning, all the pain melted away once I touched the wall. There's good, positive energy that stays with me after I've won a race. When I'm not winning, what stays with me is the pain.

***

Even with four races and four less than stellar results behind me, I still felt confident that I would win gold swimming in the 4 x 200-freestyle relay. We had a strong team. Allison Schmitt, who would lead off, was a good, young freestyler, 18 years old, and had trained with Michael and Michael's coach, Bob Bowman, with Club Wolverine at the University of Michigan. This was her first Olympics, and I knew she'd be feeling some nerves, but she was more than capable of starting us off with a great swim. Natalie Coughlin, who would swim second, was a team captain and an Olympic veteran. She had already won gold in the 100-backstroke and bronze in the 200-IM and was on her way to setting a record by winning six medals in Beijing. So she was having a great meet. Natalie and I both swam on the team that set the world record in this event at the 2007 World Championships. Caroline Burckle, another very strong freestyler, would swim the third leg, and I would finish up with the anchor leg. At this point I was faced with the reality that I would most likely leave Beijing without any individual gold medals, but I felt that if we won gold in the relay, that would be good enough. I could live with that.

Being the anchor in an Olympic 4 x 200-freestyle relay is quite stressful. You get paraded out, you get announced, and then you have to stand there for nearly six minutes watching the whole race play out in front of you before you get to dive in and swim. Being an anchor is even more stressful if things aren't unfolding as you'd hoped, and this race definitely did not unfold as I'd hoped. Allison and Natalie, our first two, didn't have great swims. We were in fifth place after the first two legs. Caroline dove in and had an awesome race. At the end of her swim, we had climbed back into third, but we were still more than three seconds behind first place Australia. I was waiting and watching all of this. Thoughts of worry filled my mind, *unless Stephanie Rice, swimming anchor for Australia, gets attacked by a shark, there's no way I'm going to be able to make up that much time.*

When I dove in, I swam right next to Jiaying Pang, the girl from China who had just beaten me in the 200-free, and the whole time I felt like I was doing terrible. I struggled to make up any time on her and felt like I was fighting all the way to the end. I touched the wall, and despite having just swum the fastest relay split of all time in this event (as I would learn later), I felt like I had failed. We finished third, behind China in second, and Australia in first. All three of the top teams went faster than what had been the world record. I looked up onto the pool deck—Allison and Caroline were pumped because they'd just won their first Olympic medals. I was devastated, but I tried to be a good teammate and look happy. In the interview line, Allison and Caroline did most of the talking. This was my last best shot at a gold, and it all just faded away. I could feel myself start to unravel. That glass full of bad water was up to the brim and starting to overflow.

They don't give you much time to wallow. I had the prelims for the 800-freestyle later that day.

✳✳✳

Under the best of circumstances, I never figured the 800-free would be a gold medal race for me, and things were far from the best of circumstances. Just about every ounce of adrenaline had drained out of me. I thrashed through my prelim. I didn't have a feel for the water. It was eight and a half minutes of pain. I finished 11th, which meant I didn't qualify for the final. I was disappointed, but to be honest, I didn't have a whole lot of emotion left. I just felt drained. No American qualified for the final, so not only had I let down myself, but I'd let down my country as well.

After you win a race, walking through the media mixed zone, where all the reporters ask you questions and the photographers take your picture, is a blast. It's the best thing ever, and really pumps you up. When you lose, it's terrible. After the 800-free, I blew past the mixed zone and said I'd talk later, but I couldn't at that moment. If I'd talked then, I would have said things I would have regretted. And Paul had vanished. I couldn't find him anywhere. I felt very abandoned at that time. His betrayal after my 400-IM was still very much on my mind. His disappearing after the 800-free was the last straw.

After the race, I went with my mom, dad, and brother to have lunch at the Omega House. While we were there a reporter came over and asked me how it felt not to have qualified for that evening's 800-free final. My dad, who is not a confrontational guy, stood up, and he was livid. We were trying to have a family lunch, and he told the reporter in no uncertain terms to leave us alone.

After the swimming events ended, we had a team wrap-up meeting, and as the meeting was breaking up, I approached Mark Schubert, the National Team head coach, and asked him if he would mediate a conversation I needed to have with Paul. I needed to tell Paul that I didn't want to work with him anymore. Mark said he would.

✶✶✶

At the 2004 Olympics, when I was 15, I went home once the swimming was over. This time I stayed. It was a bonus to be a swimmer at the Olympics because the Games last two weeks, and all of the swimming was during the first week. So then I could stay and enjoy myself without having to worry about competing the next day. I made up my mind to try to have fun. There was a lot of fun to be had.

I checked out of the Village—if I stayed in the Village, I was still bound by USA Swimming's guidelines, which are pretty strict—and Visa, one of my sponsors, put me up at a really nice hotel. There were parties everywhere, hosted by different Olympic sponsors. I just had to show my credentials to get in. I could party until 4 a.m. and then sleep until 2 p.m. the next afternoon, and then get up and do it all over again. And for some of the non-swimmers, having to compete the next day didn't stop them from partying. I remember going to a Speedo party and seeing LeBron James and Kobe Bryant and other U.S. basketball players, and they had a game the next day. That seemed insane to me, but then the U.S. basketball team won the gold medal, which was something I hadn't managed to accomplish.

It wasn't all partying—during the day I went to see some of the other sports. The president of Visa took me to the finals of women's beach volleyball, where Misty May and Keri Walsh won a gold medal. That was a blast, though I have to admit, every time I would see someone win a gold medal, it stung a little.

The closing ceremonies were bittersweet. It was a wonderful experience walking around the stadium, called The Bird's Nest because of its unique design. The Olympics is like its own little world, and now I was leaving that world, and I wasn't taking with me the things I'd come for.

They put out the Olympic Flame, and it was time to go home.

Kirsty Coventry, Stephanie Rice, and me on the podium for the 400-IM.

*My mom and me photographed years later
for the first time with all three medals on.*

PART 2

HOMECOMING

In Beijing, after our final team meeting, I approached Mark Schubert, our Olympic team head coach, and told him I needed his help. After Paul's reaction following my swim in the 400-IM, and after his no-show when I met with the media after my last race in Beijing, I had made up my mind to stop working with him. It was not an easy decision—I had been working with Paul for years, and during those years I'd become a world champion and a world record-holder—but I knew it was the right decision. I also knew that leaving him would be traumatic. And I knew that telling him I was leaving was going to be very, very difficult for me. So I asked Mark if he would be willing to mediate that conversation.

Mark agreed, and after we got back to the U.S., emails were exchanged about setting a time and a place to talk. Mark took care of the scheduling, and I was grateful for that. He asked Paul to not contact me until we had the meeting.

But before we had the meeting, I needed a break, and a vacation. My parents threw a party for me, and not long after that Brennan and I took a trip to Costa Rica. I wanted to go someplace warm, and we found a villa we really liked on the water, so off we went.

The trip didn't go well, for a number of reasons. I was paying for the whole thing—I mean, of the two of us, I was in a much better financial position to pay for the whole thing—and I think Brennan wasn't completely comfortable with that. I wasn't happy with my results in Beijing, so that put me in a bad mood. There weren't a ton of things to do at the place we stayed. Keeping busy was far more my vibe than just lounging around the pool, especially when my mind was focused on a million other things—like Beijing, or what would happen next in my career, or how I was going to have this terrible conversation with Paul.

Brennan had things on his mind, too. Paul was also his coach, and he was also thinking of leaving him, and that wasn't going to be easy for him, either. It's fair to say that I wasn't paying sufficient attention to what he was dealing with. I just wanted to talk about my own looming Paul crisis—"What if he says this? What if he says that? What should I do if this happens?" I wasn't giving Brennan what he needed, and he wasn't giving me what I needed, and we were fighting a lot. So it just didn't go well.

✶✶✶

A few days after Brennan and I returned to Baltimore, I had my conversation with Paul, with Mark mediating. Mark flew in for the meeting, and we agreed to meet at the hotel where he was staying north of the city. It didn't go well either.

First I went to the wrong hotel. I parked my car and went looking for the room number Mark had given me, but I couldn't find a room with that number. After I realized I was in the wrong place, I got back in my car and drove to the right hotel, and found the right room, and I still arrived early. So at first it was just Mark, me, my heart beating out of my chest, and this bad feeling in the pit of my stomach.

What made this so hard was that even though things with Paul weren't working out, I actually wanted them to work out. In many ways, Paul was a really good coach for me. He knew how to get me to perform my best and I had complete confidence in his workouts. We'd spent the better part of five years together. We'd achieved some amazing results. But I just felt that the trust between us, the trust that we needed between us, had been broken too many times, and I couldn't get past that. A lot of people had seen the way things had unraveled between us in Beijing. I don't think anyone was terribly surprised that I had plans to leave him, probably not even Paul himself.

We met for two hours in Mark's hotel room. The conversation went back and forth; the tension and emotions ran high. In the end, Mark made me say it. He made me say to Paul that I wanted to stop working with him and move on. That felt awful. I walked out of the meeting with my face beet red and immediately started crying. I called Brennan and my mom, and both of them came and met me and just sat with me. There wasn't a whole lot to say.

I think of myself as a forgiving person. If Paul had only apologized, if he had looked back at what had happened in Beijing and said, "Hey, I screwed up. I wasn't there for you when I should have been, and I'm sorry." If he had said that, I don't know, I might have stayed with him.

Bob Bowman, Michael's coach, was still in Michigan, but he had made plans to come back to Baltimore and NBAC. Michael had already moved back to Baltimore and was taking some time off before returning to the pool. Mark suggested that maybe I should work with Bob. In a lot of ways this made sense. Bob was a veteran coach with a good reputation, and it was hard to argue with his results—Michael had just come back from Beijing as the first person in history to win eight gold medals at a single Olympics. Besides, I'd just bought a condo and was establishing roots in Baltimore, so if I wanted to stay in Baltimore, Bob figured to be one of my very few good options. But in at least one other way, it promised to be awkward—Bob and Paul would both be coaching at the same pool, at NBAC's home base at Meadowbrook. Still, I thought the positives outweighed the negatives, so I reached out to Bob and said, "Hey, when are you coming back to Baltimore, because I need a coach."

COACH
(AND OTHER)
PROBLEMS

Later, when people asked why I moved from Paul to Bob Bowman as my coach, I would say I just needed a change of scenery, or a new challenge, or I felt like it was time to start a new chapter of my life. Blah, blah, blah...But deep down inside I knew my decision had less to do with what I was moving to, and more with what I was moving away from. The truth was that after Beijing, I needed to stop working with Paul. This felt both sad and scary, and my conviction about what I had to do bumped up against my concern that I wasn't doing the right thing. I had trusted Paul's coaching for years, and he and I had a lot of success working together. So it frightened me to pivot away from the one coach who knew me best, to a coach who didn't know a lot about me. I didn't know much about him either. Bob had put in nine highly successful years at NBAC, but since 2005 he had been at the University of Michigan, so I hadn't been around him for some time. But at least I knew him, and I trusted Mark Schubert's recommendation, so switching to Bob made the unknown I was heading into a little more known. We started working together in October of 2008.

That still left me with almost two months between the end of the Olympics and my return to the pool. After Brennan and I got back from Costa Rica, I traveled all over the place doing events for my sponsors and making other appearances. Stephanie Rice, who'd beaten me in Beijing in the 400-IM, came for a visit. We'd become good friends, and we punctuated her visit with an epic shopping trip to New York City.

Through all of this, Brennan and I drifted apart. After our complicated trip to Costa Rica, and then all of my sponsor and appearance travels, I got involved in a lot of things that didn't include him. There wasn't anyone else in my life—it was just that the distance between us grew, and we broke up.

The breakup didn't last long, maybe two months. During those months my life had settled down some, and Brennan and I had both started working out with Bob at NBAC. There were a lot of times at the pool when it would just be Bob, Brennan and me. So Brennan and I were around each other all the time, and just as we had drifted apart, we drifted back together.

Through the fall of 2008, I felt like I was in a sort of post-Beijing honeymoon period. Working with Bob went fine. I was getting back into shape and the workouts were helpful. So, for the most part, life was good. In late December, I made a bargain with Bob—I would swim an excruciating set for him if he would give me time off at New Year's to go to Las Vegas, where I'd meet Caroline Burckle and Michael and others for a big New Year's bash. He agreed, and I went and had a good time.

But part of me was struggling. The more appearances I made for my sponsors, and the more questions I got asked, the more apparent it became to the public and the media that I had not accomplished what I had been expected to in Beijing. I still had the best times in the nation in three events, but I had the crystal clear impression that others thought I failed. This weighed on me. I've always been very sensitive to what others think of me—or to what I think others think of me—and as I found myself agreeing with them and dwelling more on the traumatic side of what had happened in Beijing, I felt judged. This brought on a full-blown identity crisis and sent me down into a deep pit of depression. I started seeing a therapist for the first time in my life, at Bob's suggestion, but I didn't click with the therapist, so I quit after a few sessions.

The more the workouts ramped up, the more I struggled. When Paul was coaching me, he had done a really good job of reading me. He could tell when I was broken down, and he would back off in the workouts so I could build myself back up. With Bob it was more like, here's the workout, be tough, suck it up, and that broke me down even more. I was already in a really bad place mentally and emotionally, and it just felt like I was falling deeper and deeper into that pit, to the point where there was no way I was going to be able to climb out of it.

Michael came back to NBAC in January 2009, and soon afterwards controversy erupted. He hadn't been back for long when there was a big media blowup after unfortunate photos of him at a campus party got published. So now Michael struggled with the fallout from that, and Bob became preoccupied with Michael, and reporters swarmed around the NBAC pool, and my head wasn't in the right place, and it just felt like everything that could go wrong was going wrong. No one was at their best, to put it mildly, and the environment we were floundering in had turned toxic.

Meanwhile, the workouts kept breaking me down. After Athens in 2004, I worked hard to build my confidence back up. That wasn't happening now. I swam terribly in workouts. When I dove in the pool, I didn't feel like I had the instincts I once had. I cried every day, it was the snowball effect of all of these things.

Bob's coaching philosophy was different from Paul's. Bob's approach—and there are a lot of coaches like this—was to pile on the yardage and the weight training throughout the season, and then taper off a few weeks before big meets, like Nationals or Worlds or Olympic Trials. The idea was that then you'd swim your best times at these big meets. This worked well for a lot of swimmers. Michael responded well to it. It worked well for Brennan. It didn't work as well for me though. I had never experienced this approach, and it was hard for me to trust that even though I might be swimming 10 seconds slower than my best time in practice, once I tapered everything would work out fine, and my times would magically drop. I just felt beaten down. Paul's workouts may have been intense, but he wanted me to train fast, and his workouts weren't designed to wear me down to the point where it felt impossible to train fast.

It wasn't just Bob's coaching philosophy, his coaching style was different. He liked to yell, and when he would yell at me it would be a trigger—a sense that my coach was questioning my effort or my integrity. I'm a very self-motivating person. I was always dialed in. I was always focused. I was always ready to go. I didn't need a coach on my butt yelling at me. So, Bob would yell, and I would crumble, and then I would go off and cry and come back. After Beijing, I was in a pretty vulnerable place. Maybe I wasn't as mentally tough as I needed to be but yelling at me didn't help. It just made me feel worse about myself.

Again, in fairness, this approach worked with others. The screaming matches that Bob and Michael could get into became legendary, and Michael seemed to thrive off of this. Brennan seemed okay with Bob's style, too. It just didn't work for me.

This whole time, Bob was working with a group of seven or eight of us, and Paul was right there working with another group of NBAC swimmers. So that was awkward. When Paul and I would walk past each other on the pool deck, we may have exchanged some gesture of acknowledgment, but no words were spoken. One afternoon, as a prank, Michael threw all of the things from my mesh bag into the pool. He may have meant it as a joke—sort of like he'd done when he filled my mesh bag with orange peels once before—but as I went in the pool to fish my things out of the water, I felt humiliated and embarrassed.

While this scenario unfolded, Paul and I exchanged a look—I don't know if he felt sorry for me or thought that I'd gotten what I deserved for leaving him, but we had this moment.

Around this time, through the early months of 2009, I was competing okay—not great, but okay. I usually finished in the top three in my races, but I wasn't experiencing the same feelings of dominance that I'd felt in 2008, in the lead-up to Beijing, where every time I got in the pool, and no matter what happened in the race, I felt confident that I could beat the people I swam against. I had lost that. I didn't feel any easy speed. I didn't feel any pop. I didn't feel great about myself. I just tried to push through and be tough. If I felt low, I swam low, and I felt about as low as I could feel. I lived by myself at this point, and some days my mom came over just to be with me and provide support. I cried so much that I would hyperventilate.

Others also noticed the change in me, even if they didn't know the reasons. "You just weren't the same person," Brennan told me later. "You didn't have that same way about you when you were in the water."

In 2009, all of our work was in preparation for the World Championships scheduled for Rome in late July and early August. In the spring, we had the fiasco in California where we "pretended" we were Navy SEALs for a day, and, early in the summer, we went to training camp at the Olympic Training Center. Ordinarily this would be a great time in our preparation. But I went in feeling sad and depleted, and I just got buried. We did triples—three workouts a day, or four if you counted weight training. At one point I texted Bob and told him I was done. I was crying every day, my self-esteem had drained out, and I wanted to quit. But my identity was so wrapped up in my swimming that the next day I changed my mind. I came back to practice and swam. I didn't know what else to do.

We went straight from Colorado Springs to California, to the Santa Clara Grand Prix, and I got sick. I was coughing nonstop and had a fever. My dad flew out from Baltimore and moved me in with my aunt and uncle, who lived nearby. I stayed with them for three days and missed most of the meet.

After Santa Clara, we went back to Baltimore to get ready for the World Championship Trials, slated for Indianapolis in early July, which would double as the U.S. Nationals. At this point it was obvious to everyone, Bob included, that I had become a shadow of my former world record-holding self. A couple of weeks before World Championship Trials, we had a practice at Meadowbrook where we put on our racing suits and pretended we were swimming in an actual meet. My times improved, but then it turned out they weren't really my times. Bob had made them up, in an attempt to boost my confidence, which was so low at that point that faking my times might have been exactly what I needed. But Michael found out what Bob was doing and told me I wasn't swimming the times I thought I was. Bob overheard Michael and just exploded, and the two of them had this major blowup right there on the pool deck.

After Beijing I swore off individual medley, so at trials I only swam freestyle. I swam four events—the 100-, 200-, 400-, and 800-freestyle—and all went terribly. I swam 10 seconds slower than my best time in the 400-free and finished seventh. I swam four or five seconds slower in the 200-free. The whole meet was a disaster. The water felt like molasses. After I got out of the pool, a cameraman followed me; I stepped behind a curtain to get away from him. I didn't want my picture taken, because a picture of me at that point would have been a picture of failure. I had gone from breaking world records in 2008 to not even qualifying for the World Championship team a year later.

✶✶✶

After trials, the U.S. team went to training camp, without me, and then off to Rome for the World Championships. When they came home, I went into Bob's office at Meadowbrook and told him I had to get out. At trials I had been the most miserable I had been in my entire life. I had to leave NBAC and figure out my next step. He was understanding and professional, and I don't think I surprised him. Our meeting lasted all of three and a half minutes.

I had actually made up my mind to leave weeks before, and I wasn't leaving into a void. The U.S. Olympic Committee was talking about forming a team in California, and Caroline Burckle and I decided to join. While the U.S. National Team was in Rome at the World Championships, I went to California to go house hunting.

CALIFORNIA

Jack Roach is kind of the wise old owl of American swimming. He spent years on the coaching staff of USA Swimming, and in 2008 was the head coach for USA Swimming's National Junior Team. It seems like he's always been around in the swimming world, and I've known him for years. In 2009, when it felt like the wheels were coming off for me professionally and personally, he became a really close confidant. Throughout that time, I put all the blame on myself, telling myself I was weak, or not tough enough. Trying day after day and failing day after day had taken its toll on my sense of self. He'd kept an eye on my career from afar for years, and in 2009 he stepped in more directly.

That summer, when I was at the Olympic Training Center for camp in Colorado Springs, Jack and I went for coffee at the Broadmoor Hotel, one day. He was the first person who helped me understand that maybe the problems I was struggling with weren't all about me, that maybe I was just in a situation that wasn't a good fit for me, and that maybe I needed a change. I felt empowered. I felt—I feel—grateful. My conversation with Jack had a lot to do with my decision to move to California in September 2009.

Caroline Burckle and I rented a house together in a nice neighborhood in Newport Beach, about 30 minutes from the pools of the Fullerton Aquatics Sports Team, or FAST, home of this new team we had joined. It meant a lot to me to be roommates with Caroline. This was my first real experience living on my own away from my parents, and it helped to learn to be independent but with the support of someone who was a good friend. We shopped at Trader Joe's together. On Sundays, we watched Desperate Housewives together. We did all the normal things you do when you settle into a new place. Caroline was looking for her own fresh start, and we became each other's support network.

FAST was one of several training centers funded by USA Swimming and the U.S. Olympic Committee to work with elite swimmers. A big part of what attracted me to it was the opportunity to work with the two coaches who would be in charge. One was Jon Urbanchek, who was a legend in the swimming world. Jon, then in his early 70s, had recently retired after more than 20 years as head swimming coach at the University of Michigan, winning 13 Big Ten Championships in the process. He was widely respected in the swimming world, known for pushing swimmers hard into different heart rate zones. He color-coded those heart rate zones and became known for that. Jon is also one of the kindest human beings I've ever met. But if I had just worked with him, I ran a very strong risk of getting beaten down again, in much the same way I had with Bob. The other coach, Sean Hutchison, had a reputation as an innovator. He was meticulous about technique—his warmups could take an hour—and in his workouts, he placed more emphasis on speed and swimming at race pace. They each had their strengths, and I thought working with the two of them together would be the perfect balance.

That perfect balance didn't materialize as I'd hoped. We started swimming in the early fall with Sean, and for months it was just Sean—Jon hadn't arrived yet. Then even after Jon arrived, our group—there were maybe eight of us—just kept working with only Sean well into 2010. Jon's group and Sean's group practiced separately. I'm not sure why this happened, but it wasn't what I had expected.

✳✳✳

A few months into 2010, Brennan and I broke up. He was in college in Baltimore at Loyola University, and I was 2,700 miles away in California. We were just too far apart to sustain a relationship.

✳✳✳

In some ways, 2010 looked like a comeback year for me. A year after failing to qualify for the World Championships, I won the 400-freestyle at the U.S. Nationals in August in Irvine, California, and took third in the 200-free. But my times weren't great. I was three seconds off my best time in the 400-free, and I wasn't feeling like I'd come all the way back. My results were good enough to qualify for the 2011 Worlds, but I didn't feel like the dominant person and confident swimmer I'd been in 2008. It was better than rock bottom, but I was still wondering, *who am I? Who is this person who feels so different from just a few years ago?*

So I had not totally recovered. I wasn't feeling like myself. My self-esteem was off. But then good things happened. I ended up getting selected for the 2010 Short Course World Championships that December in Dubai, and I had an awesome meet.

I won the 400-free and finished second in both the 200-free and the 4 x 100-freestyle relay (an event I hardly ever swam). Sean had us doing power work and focused more on what we were doing underwater, and that really paid off in the 25-meter pool. The results also earned me some good prize money. I felt redeemed, almost like my old self again.

Feeling on top of the world at the 2010
Short Course World Championships in Dubai.

The meet in Dubai ended a week before Christmas. Afterward I flew to Baltimore to spend some time with my family before flying back to California to see Caroline, who had retired after the 2010 Nationals and moved to Santa Monica. In late December, when I was with Caroline in Santa Monica, the news popped; rumors circulated that Sean Hutchison was having a relationship with one of his female swimmers on FAST. He denied the rumors but resigned from FAST in December. Just like that, he was gone from the pool deck.

The news in 2010 sent the swimming world spinning. Rumors and speculation swirled around who the female swimmer might have been, but at that point they were just that—rumors and speculation. For me personally, I had just spent over a year working to adjust to Sean as my coach, and now this had happened. With him gone, Jon would be my only coach.

Seven years later, Ariana Kukors, one of my FAST teammates, who had worked with Sean since her early teens, went public with accusations that he had sexually abused her.

✶✶✶

Having Jon Urbanchek as my only coach may not have been ideal—I worried that his workouts would beat me down—but given a choice between Jon and Sean, I would have gone with Jon every time. I had already been planning to make the move to his group. With Sean out of the picture, Jon's group included me, two other girls, and a lot of guys, so it was very much a boys' environment. I would get teased, and I would tease back, and while it was mostly in good fun, sometimes it was too much for me. There were days when I would drive home from practice in tears, over-analyzing how I'd reacted to their teasing. I mostly kept that to myself.

This all took place at the beginning of 2011, about six months out from World Championships, which was not a time when you want to have a lot of changes in your routine. The mini glow I felt after my success at the Short Course Worlds in Dubai faded. I never really felt like things had fallen into place.

✶✶✶

For the rest of 2011, I wasn't my best self. At training camp for Worlds, I was beaten down and cried a lot. Jon is such a sweet man, and he'd reach out to me, but that just made me think that all of my teammates resented me because they probably thought he babied me, and even though I was grateful to Jon for reaching out, I felt guilty for needing that kind of support. I was in that vortex again—a spiraling disaster of low self-esteem and no confidence. Looking back on it all, I think I never really took the time I needed to heal from either the trauma of Beijing in 2008 or the storm that was 2009. My approach was to just keep going. I was a professional athlete—it was my job to keep going. But I hadn't truly grasped what those two years had done to my psyche, to my own definition of who I was as a person.

The 2011 World Championships were in Shanghai, and my results were mixed. I swam the 4 x 200-freestyle relay with Missy Franklin, Dagny Knutson, and Allison Schmitt, and we took gold. In the 400-free, I finished seventh. After all of my races were over, I went to a restaurant in Shanghai with my mom and I told her I wanted to be done. I said, "I am not myself, I am miserable, and no matter how much I keep trying to push forward, things aren't getting any better." But I talked it over more with her and I talked things over with Peter Carlisle, my agent, and once again I changed my mind. I decided that with a year to go until the 2012 Olympics, I wanted to keep going.

✶✶✶

I went straight from Shanghai to Palo Alto for the U.S. National Championships. I wanted to swim some more events and try to improve my rankings. But when our plane landed in Palo Alto, I felt very average. I swam okay, but apparently this was the new normal. Four years earlier, in the lead up to Beijing, it was all very exciting. I swam my best and I felt more than ready to take on the world. Now I felt, *oh, God. I have another whole year to go?* That wasn't the best attitude to have.

Near the end of 2011, I went to training camp in again. Paul was there. He had left NBAC not long after I did, going first to become an assistant swimming coach at the University of Auburn and then going to Naples, Florida, to coach a new team called T2 Aquatics. He was in Colorado Springs with T2. Our relationship had evolved over the years, and, at this point, we were in a pretty good place with each other. We would run into each other at meets from time to time, and at Nationals in California the year before; he had congratulated me for swimming well. We had both kind of moved on. When I saw him in Colorado Springs, I asked him if we could get together to talk, and we ended up meeting at a Chinese restaurant outside of the training center. We talked for over an hour, both of us avoiding any mention of our ugly breakup three years earlier. I asked him if I could come swim with him at T2, and he said yes.

I told Jon Urbanchek I was going to leave FAST. It was important to me that I had his blessing. He said he understood and wished me good luck.

FLORIDA

I had forgiven Paul for what had happened in Beijing in 2008, but I hadn't forgotten. My hope was, *okay, it's been three years, we've put that behind us and we're ready to move on.* I had completely changed as a person, so maybe he had too, and maybe the whole coach-swimmer thing between us could end on a positive note. I had swum the best in my life when I worked with him. It could be the fairytale ending. I would make the Olympic team again. I would do well in London at the Olympics, cue the happy music. Besides, I didn't really have the luxury of worrying about my past. I had eight months to get ready, and if I was going to make the U.S. team, I needed to be in a very different place from the one I was in when I left California for Florida. T2 may not have looked like the answer to everyone around me. My mom, in particular, wondered what in the world I was doing, but this was the answer for me.

The workouts I did with Paul at T2 may have been geared to a somewhat older me—I would turn 23 in 2012, right before the Olympic Trials—but they were very much in line with what we used to do, and we were still really hitting high-level paces. I had been a machine at 18, and I could crank through workouts that were insane. Four years later I was different. I didn't feel old for a swimmer, I was 18 years younger than Dara Torres when she qualified for the 2008 Games as a 41-year-old mother, but I wasn't the same person I'd been in 2008. I didn't have the same momentum or the same confidence. I had just moved my life across the country, and if I had felt great in California, I wouldn't have done that.

At T2, Paul had a good group. Erika Erndl, whose husband Kevin had started T2 (and recruited Paul), was an older swimmer, aiming to make her first Olympic team at age 34. Erika had swum at her first Olympic Trials in 1996 (when I was seven). Eighteen-year-old Elizabeth Pelton had come from NBAC; she had moved to Florida to join Paul at T2 and spent her senior year of high school living with Erika and Kevin. Bridget Halligan was coming off of a standout career swimming at the University of South Carolina, where she set all kinds of school records. About six weeks before trials, she and I started meeting at the beach where we would just sit and talk and watch the sunset. She gave me a lot of support before, during, and after trials.

My training went about the best it had gone in a year or more. I was hitting good paces. I didn't feel the same as I had felt when I was 18 or 19, but for the most part I felt good. I was swimming solid times at meets. I liked the women I was swimming with, Naples was fun, and we were training outdoors in this beautiful place. Overall it was a very positive experience. I thought, *okay, here we go. I'm getting it back. This is great.*

But this feeling that things were going well was fleeting. I'd go to one meet and do okay, and then go to another and just completely fall apart. That extra gear I used to count on had become unreliable. I was only just starting to build my confidence back up, and with only six months until trials, I just wasn't sure there was enough time.

✳✳✳

The 2012 Olympic Trials were held in late June and early July at the CenturyLink Center in Omaha, the same pool where I'd set a world record four years earlier. We got there a few days ahead of time, and I felt strong in my warmups in the days before the races started. I had some nervousness, but nothing unusual. I was scheduled to swim four events—the 100-, 200-, 400-, and 800-meter freestyle. The 400-free would come first, on day two. Not having to swim the 400-individual medley on day one was awesome. I stayed in the hotel to rest and watched the races on TV. But that day I started to feel a wobbly, shaky feeling all over my body. I shook it off and went to bed early to be ready for the 400-free the next day.

I woke up on day two and immediately knew something was wrong. Kevin Erndl drove us in the van to the pool, and I told him my stomach felt weird. He said it might just be nerves, but I thought, *no, it's not.* Nervousness had never manifested itself that way with me before, and at this point in my career, I wasn't a rookie—I could tell the difference between nerves and illness. I'd been eating at restaurants and ordering take-out since arriving in Omaha, and something wasn't settling right. I felt weak, queasy, and nauseous, and it felt like there was a rock in my stomach. I couldn't eat anything—even the thought of eating felt repulsive.

The 400-free was the last event of the day. I sat around waiting with everything swirling around me, hoping I'd feel better, but thought, *oh, this is not good.*

It wasn't good. In my prelim I felt helpless, with no power behind my strokes. I swam nowhere near my best time and didn't qualify for the finals.

"Falling ill at the Olympic Trials or Olympic Games is any athlete's nightmare," wrote a reporter covering the trials for *Swimming World* magazine, "and Hoff is unfortunately living the experience."

I just wanted to go back to the hotel and hit reset, to get ready for the 200-free the next day. I felt like I needed to eat something, so I ordered a bowl of French onion soup. Big mistake. It was the first time I'd eaten French onion soup, and also the last. My whole body felt weak. I broke out in cold sweats.

The nightmare continued the next day into the 200-free. I had the same feeling—helpless and weak. I swam three seconds slower than what I'd already done that season, and I felt humiliated and confused. At this point I thought I was done.

The 800-free was a few days later, and by that time I still wasn't my normal self, but I felt a little bit better. I debated with Paul whether to do the race—under the best of circumstances, I figured to be a long shot to make the team in this event—and he was very supportive, saying he would be fine with whatever I decided. I remember talking with Davis Tarwater from the men's team, a good friend who went on to win a gold medal in a relay at that year's Olympics. I had thought about retiring if I didn't make the Olympic team, and Davis knew this, and he said to me that if I didn't swim the 800, I'd regret ending my career that way. That rang true. The race didn't go well, but I'm glad I swam it. Afterwards, Paul went with me when I met with the media, and then he walked me back to my hotel.

I needed some time off. I wasn't ready to announce that I was retiring, but I wasn't sure I wasn't going to retire, either. I was ready to end this chapter, but not ready to close the book.

TODD

If 2012 has a silver lining, it's that, despite my high hopes and eventual disappointment in the pool, I met Todd Anderson, the man who is now my husband. Todd played football at Michigan State, and had a goal of playing in the NFL. We met in Naples, Florida, where he had gone to train with a group of other football players with similar aspirations.

At the time, I was dating a different football player, even though I didn't know much about football. I had this stereotype of football players that they were all pretty full of themselves. A group of us had gone out one night to a bar, went dancing, and had a lot of fun. Todd was one of the people in that group. The next morning, we all went out for breakfast, and I got to talk to him some more. I remember at breakfast he teased me about something I'd put on Twitter. So, I thought, *this guy who I just met is following me on Twitter?* He was really funny.

Todd was only in Florida for a couple of months, and then he went back to East Lansing and Michigan State for his Pro Day, when NFL scouts go to college campuses to look at prospects. Meanwhile I stayed in Naples to train for the Olympic Trials. Todd got picked up by the Rams (they were the St. Louis

Rams then), and I sent him a message congratulating him. He messaged back, thanking me, and asking how my training was going. So now we were communicating back and forth between East Lansing and Naples, as friends. He said he looked forward to following me at trials and asked if I could send him a Speedo shirt to wear while he watched on TV, so he could sort of rep Speedo for me. I said, sure, although getting a Speedo shirt in XXL wasn't easy. That's not a normal thing. Very few guy swimmers are XXL.

"Who is this girl?" his mom said to him when the Speedo shirt arrived. "I think she likes you."

✳✳✳

Not many people understand what it's like to train four years for something—four very up and down years, in my case—and then see the thing you've been training for just washed down the drain in a few days' time. They'd say, "Hey, it's okay," or "Don't worry—it'll all work out for the best," or "You tried your hardest." Those were about the worst things they could say to me. It's not okay. It won't "work out." That wasn't my best, and even if it was, it wasn't good enough.

Like they'd done for 2008, my whole family came to Omaha for the Olympic Trials, only this time instead of celebrating my wins in five races, we didn't even watch the finals. We were off someplace getting ice cream, and I felt miserable about not making the Olympic team. Then a text dinged my phone, and it was from Todd in Michigan, that read, "Thoughts and prayers are with you," with three purple hearts. And I thought, *okay, this guy gets it*.

After I went back to Florida, he invited me to visit him in Michigan for a couple of days before he went to the Rams' camp. I said I would. It would not have been healthy for me to stay home alone by myself in Florida at that time. I flew first to Seattle to see a former roommate, Tressa Grummer (now

Solovy), who I met in California when I was taking courses at Chapman University. From there, I went to Michigan. When the plane landed, I thought, *what am I doing? I've seen this guy maybe twice in my life. I barely know him. And now I'm flying to his college town to visit him?*

We ended up having an awesome weekend. I told him things that I hadn't told anyone else, except family, about how I felt about swimming. It felt like we could talk forever. We just clicked.

✳✳✳

I was in California visiting my friend Ed Moses when the London Olympics started. Ed is another swimmer who had won gold and silver medals at the 2000 Olympics in Sydney. Caroline Burckle and I had become friends with Ed when we were roommates in Newport Beach. The Olympics were going to be hard for me to watch, but Elizabeth Beisel was swimming the 400-IM and Allison Schmitt was swimming in the 400-free. They were both good friends of mine, and I wanted to see them swim. Before the race, NBC ran a clip of my 400-freestyle finish from Beijing in 2008, the race where I got out-touched and missed gold by seven hundredths of a second. It was the first time I'd seen the video since watching it from the pool deck in Beijing, and I just lost it. I broke down crying. Ed gave me exactly the kind of support I needed in that moment, including a consoling hug.

✳✳✳

After I left California, I flew back to Naples. Todd was in St. Louis, at the Rams' training camp, trying to make the team as a fullback, and things weren't going well for him. He'd injured his hamstring, and he was on the bubble—he could either make the team, or if the bubble burst, get cut. I wanted to do something to help. I called his mom—a cold call, we hadn't met, and I didn't know her. She was heading to St. Louis to see Todd's preseason game against the Kansas City Chiefs. I asked her if she thought it would be a good distraction or a bad distraction if I flew out for a visit. On the call I referred to myself as Todd's "friend," but she knew there was more to it than that. She said I should come. When I got to the airport in Fort Myers, I texted Todd a picture of me standing at my gate with the words "St. Louis boarding." His mom was with him when he got the text. She said he looked

confused, then very happy.

The deal was, if the Rams lost to the Chiefs, the players had to return to camp and all the restrictions that went with it. If they beat the Chiefs, Todd would have some free time. The Rams beat the Chiefs. The next day, Todd and I celebrated with a date at the Melting Pot. Todd managed to spill an entire glass of water on himself. As tempting as it might be to write this off as new relationship nerves, that's just Todd. More than once I've heard his parents say he's a bull in a china shop.

After their last preseason game, the Rams cut Todd. I had flown back to Naples, but after the Rams let him go, I flew back to Michigan to spend time with him at his parents' house in Jackson. He had the option of becoming a free agent and seeing if another team would pick him up, but he was tired of being injured and tired of the "bouncing around" life he was living. He decided it was time to hang up the proverbial cleats. I canceled my flight back to Naples, and he and I drove the 19 hours back to Florida so he could move in with me. When we were about three or four hours from Naples, things got really quiet in the car. We had known each other for just a couple of months. We had been officially dating for three or four weeks. I think we were both thinking, *this is risky. What did we just do?*

It's all so serendipitous—who you meet, who you like, who you wind up agreeing to spend the rest of your life with. I knew there was something special about Todd because of the text he sent me to console me after my disastrous 2012 Olympic Trials. It's strange how these things work out, but if I had never gotten a stomach bug, if I had swum great at trials, if I had gone on to make the 2012 Olympic team and gone to London, there's a pretty good chance we wouldn't be married today.

BLOOD CLOTS

Not long after we arrived in Naples, Derek Touchette, a football friend of Todd's (he trained Todd for his Pro Day), got him a job as a fitness training intern at a facility he ran. My future, however, remained very much in doubt. I had maybe four months left on the lease for my place in Naples, and after that...what? Go back to California? Keep swimming? Quit swimming? Finish my degree? Meanwhile, Todd and I were in the middle of this crash course in figuring each other out. We're both passionate and stubborn people, and when you put two people like that together, you can get some intense fights. Our relationship sounds a little like a fairytale, but that period of time when we first moved in together was hard. The best fairytales have their dark side.

I decided to go back to school in 2013 at the University of Miami, which had strong programs in the fields I was interested in, like communications, marketing, public relations, and business. This meant moving to Miami, and for Todd it meant moving there without a job. Once again, it didn't take him long to find one, as a personal trainer at the South Beach location of the fitness company Equinox.

In January, an article in *Swimming World* magazine announced that I'd retired from swimming. Todd and I had gone to Michigan for Christmas, and when we boarded our plane back to Florida, I left my phone on a seat in the Detroit airport, so I didn't learn about this until after we landed. I was furious! It turned out to be a misunderstanding, based on a conversation a reporter had with Paul. *How could my "retirement" be announced without anyone talking to me about it?* I sent out a Tweet to set the record straight:

"To clarify, I am not retired. I am taking some time to go to school at the University of Miami and focus on my studies."

If I was going to keep open the option of returning to competition, I needed to stay in shape, so I started lifting weights and swam with the university club team. My workouts were a little inconsistent, but they were better than nothing. If I decided to go back to swimming, I didn't want to have to start from scratch.

In the spring of 2013, I got a call from Jack Roach. He had been named head coach of the U.S. Junior World Championship team that would compete in Dubai in August, and he wanted to know if I would be interested in joining him as an athlete mentor. I wasn't sure what to say. The kids who compete in the Junior Worlds are young—some are as young as 14 or 15, and no one is older than 18—and I didn't know what they'd think about being mentored by someone who hadn't even made the Olympic team in 2012. I went back and forth on it, but ultimately, I said yes.

It was both uplifting and frustrating to be around those kids. It was uplifting to see the energy and enthusiasm they brought to what for many was their first international competition. One of the athletes was Kathleen Baker, who went on to win gold at the 2016 Olympics in the 4x100 medley relay. Another was Caeleb Dressel, who won two golds in Rio and who some predicted might be the next Michael Phelps. It was frustrating because I wanted to be out there in the pool with them. Watching these kids kind of ignited my spark a little bit.

Andy Kershaw had been hired as head coach at the University of Miami. I'd known Andy for years, and I really liked the way he coached. After I returned from Dubai, I approached him and said, "Hey, I'm thinking of giving this another shot. What do you think?" He was on board with the idea, and in the fall of 2013, I started working out with the university club team on a more consistent basis.

My comeback had ups and downs to it, but overall it went well. I kept building momentum, and I kept building confidence. Working with Andy felt like a breath of fresh air. For the first time in my career, my relationship to my coach was a real partnership. I was a veteran swimmer at a point in my career where I knew a lot about what I needed to do, so Andy and I collaborated in creating my workouts.

After a couple of months working with Andy, I entered my first meet, a super local meet with age groups down to 9-10 and 11-12. Every time I would climb out of the water the little kids would flock over and ask for my autograph. Todd went with me. He's a big guy and looks massive on a pool deck. The kids thought he was my bodyguard.

Everything we did was geared toward getting me prepared for the National Championships in August 2014 in Irvine, California. And everything we did made sense—the strength work, the dryland workouts, the pool workouts, the benchmarks we set. I built myself back up slowly, but by the summer I felt really good about Andy and really good about myself. And I was enjoying the process.

At the last meet before Nationals, a sectional meet in Orlando, I took maybe two seconds off my best time ever in the 100-breaststroke, and I swam right at my best times for the season in the 200-freestyle. The morning we were to leave for Irvine I swam paces for the 200-IM that were probably the best I'd done since 2008. I had been dialed in to every aspect of training more than I ever had been. I was so excited, ready to crush it. I thought, *I am about to light up this comeback, and Nationals is going to be my coming out party.*

✮✮✮

In Orlando, after the sectional meet, I had felt soreness in my calf and also around my ribs. I didn't think much of it, just wrote it off to the soreness I'd always get day in and day out from hard training. Then when we landed in California for Nationals I felt this weirdness in my chest, kind of like how you feel when a cold is coming on. Again, I tried to put it out of my mind.

But whatever was going on wasn't getting better. Warming up in the pool in Irvine, I was having trouble with the distance I wanted to go underwater—I felt like I needed to come up sooner than I wanted to. I just couldn't get enough air. This was weird, and new, but I decided it was just a reaction to the flight. I told myself, *I cannot get sick right now, so I'm going to ignore this.* I still had two days before the 100-free, which I had planned as a sort of "get the first race out of the way" swim, to help me prepare for the 200-free on day two.

On Tuesday, the day before the 100-free, I had a strange ache in my rib area. I called Todd—he was going to fly to California that night—and I told him something weird was going on, that I felt this tightness in my chest, but I was pretty sure if I just took some Advil it would go away.

I woke up Wednesday morning and I panicked, the pain was worse. I assumed it was a muscle strain, but for the life of me I couldn't figure out how I would have strained it. For 75 meters, my 100-freestyle race went fine, but in the final 25, I had no air. I got out of the pool and felt searing pain. I couldn't breathe deeply. I hadn't made the top 16, so I wasn't going to advance. With time, the pain lessened some, and I took it easy that afternoon. I figured, *okay, let's put this one behind us, move on, and get ready for the 200-free.*

That evening I went to dinner with Andy and Todd, and in the middle of dinner I started having spasms. It felt like somebody was stabbing me in the ribs with a sword, over and over. I went to the bathroom and just started crying. I texted Todd, and he came in and got me from the bathroom and took me to see a doctor. It's interesting, looking back that the doctor that night raised the possibility of it being a blood clot, but then he wrote off that idea because it was such a remote chance, given my history as an athlete. Ultimately, he decided I had an intercostal strain, which is a strain of the muscles that connect your ribs. He gave me some anti-inflammatories and advised me to rest.

That night the spasms intensified, and I woke up crying and holding my side. I couldn't breathe—I couldn't take in air, it was so painful, and eventually I passed out, fortunately landing on the bed instead of something less forgiving. Todd and Andy tried to figure out what to do. Eventually the pain subsided some, and I came to, but it was the scariest and most painful time of my life.

I scratched the 200-free, though I still held out hope that I would recover by day five to swim the 200-IM. Over the next few days I got a cortisone shot, and we went to the Equinox in Irvine so I could get a massage and soak in their hot tub. Again, at this point we were still working on the premise that it was a muscle strain, and not something more serious, and it just seemed silly that I couldn't push through a muscle strain. On day four, I got in the water, and I had problems just trying to take in air. I swam maybe four laps and stopped. Andy and Todd looked down at me from the pool deck, trying to be supportive. I looked up and said, "One of you is going to have to tell me to get out of the water, because I know if I get out, it's over." Both of their faces were filled with sadness. They said, "Yeah, we think you should get out of the water." So, we scratched the 200-IM and flew home.

✻✻✻

Back in Miami, I went to a doctor who said I had pneumonia. *Okay, I can live with that. It's treatable.* It's better than an intercostal strain, which, can take six months to recover from. But meanwhile, I could still barely lay on my back because of the pain. I went to another doctor who had me do breathing exercises with a weight on my chest. (That wasn't fun.) I went to the Mount Sinai Medical Center, to the hospital at the University of Miami, looking for answers, advice, and help. I began to question not only my toughness, but my sanity.

Six weeks after the symptoms started, I finally got to see my primary care doctor. In all of this time, no one had done a blood test, so I asked for…actually I demanded one. I had elevated D-dimer, which can indicate a blood clot. The doctor ordered a CAT scan at Mount Sinai. The scan showed two blood clots in the bottom of my lungs. "We need to admit you," he said, "so get in this wheelchair."

Was I concerned by this news? Sure. Blood clots are dangerous, and you don't expect to see them in someone who's in great shape and 25 years old. But mostly I was relieved. Finally, finally, after all the pain and the spasms and the difficulty breathing and the tests—finally things made sense.

FIRST PITCH

Sandwiched between these two dark times in my life—my failure to qualify for the London Olympics and the diagnosis of blood clots in my lungs—came one unexpected and totally delightful bright spot.

While Todd and I were living in Miami, we had gotten to be good friends with Randy Frankel, who was part-owner of the Tampa Bay Rays. Randy worked out at Equinox, where Todd worked, so we got to know him through that. Randy is a great guy, and one of the most generous and down-to-earth people you'll meet. Todd had an idea. He asked Randy if he could arrange for me to throw out the first pitch at a Rays game in the spring of 2014. Randy agreed to help, and they picked a weekend game when the Rays would play against the Yankees, so there figured to be a big crowd. I was nervous—throwing baseballs is not my thing, so I would need to practice to avoid embarrassing myself. Todd knew I'd be preoccupied with practicing, and that played into his plans.

The game was on Sunday, April 20, an afternoon game. We drove over to Tampa on Friday, and I had to get permission from Andy to miss practice. I got in a workout Sunday morning at a pool in Tampa, to keep him (and me) happy. All of this was happening about a week before the Grand Prix in Mesa, Arizona, where I was going to launch my comeback. I couldn't afford to miss a workout.

For the game, Randy had a Rays jersey made for me with "HOFF" in capital letters on the back. I practiced with one of the Rays pitchers, worried I wouldn't be able to throw straight. I was so focused. As it got closer to the time when I was supposed to take the mound, I looked around for Todd, but couldn't find him, which was annoying because I wanted his support.

So now I was on. The announcer ran through a list of accolades, and I smiled and waved to the crowd. The Rays mascot, a big, blue furry creature named "Raymond," set up to be my catcher, and I started to focus on him, or it, or whatever.

Watch him get down on one knee!

Then I listened to the announcer, and he was talking about Todd. He was talking about our first date, when Todd spilled water on himself. *What in the world is going on? Why is this guy talking about Todd?* The next thing I knew Todd ran in from the outfield and handed me a big bouquet of roses. I didn't figure out what was going on until he dropped to one knee. And that was it—Todd proposed. In the surprise and shock of it all, I don't even remember saying "yes," though it was pretty obvious to everyone there—and now to the tens of thousands of people who have watched it on YouTube—that my answer was "yes."

Todd had concocted the whole thing—with Andy, with Randy, with my parents, with his parents, with our friends— everybody knew what was going on but me. Todd had flown his parents and my mom to Tampa (my dad had a work commitment and couldn't come). They stayed in the same hotel Todd and I were in, on the same floor even, just down the hall from us. Todd's good friend Marc Megna, a former pro football player, helped with the organizing, and even ran Todd through kneeling exercises so he would get the proposal right. Todd had arranged this whole elaborate warning system with text messages so I wouldn't run into anybody I wasn't supposed to know was there.

Of course, after the proposal I still had to throw out the first pitch. Todd replaced the furry blue mascot and squatted down to play catcher. I threw straight, but the ball bounced once in front of home plate before it reached him. Ugh!

We watched the game from Randy's box, and everyone was there. It was a huge surprise and so special.

✳✳✳

Four days later we were in Arizona, for the Mesa Grand Prix, where I was scheduled to swim five events. I had a good meet, and won the 200-individual medley, though it was stressful trying to figure out where I could safely put my engagement ring when I was in the pool. It was great to feel like I was back, to win a race, and to be engaged to the man I love.

Grand Prix win fueled by love.

✳✳✳

Then came the blood clots, a few months later at Nationals. I started taking blood thinners to treat them (Xarelto, in particular, and full disclosure, I have done promotional work for them—more on this later). I tried later to mount yet another comeback—I had been selected to compete at the Short Course World Championships—but I still didn't feel right. The blood clots had been in my body long enough to leave scar tissue behind, so that explained part of the problem, but not all of it. I wasn't experiencing the sharp pains that I had before, but I still couldn't get enough air. I was sure something else was wrong.

The thymus gland is a walnut-sized organ located behind your breastbone that plays a role in regulating the immune system. It's supposed to get smaller after you hit puberty, but mine was getting larger—it was twice as big as it should have been, big enough that for a while doctors were concerned I might have some type of cancer. They decided that mine should be removed.

The surgery wasn't super invasive, but recovery was rough and painful. I woke up in the intensive care unit at Mount Sinai hospital with two big tubes coming out of my side. Andy came to visit me, and I celebrated his visit by throwing up into a pan. When the tubes were removed, it felt like my insides were being ripped out. Stuff was leaking out of me. It was not a pleasant scene.

I've often wondered if there was some correlation between the blood clots and the problem with my thymus gland, but nobody seems to know for sure.

The surgery was successful. After you reach a certain age, you don't really need your thymus gland, and I was well past that age. My hope was that after the surgery, the doctors would tell me that I was going to be back to my normal self. That's not what happened. I remember I was in a grocery store one afternoon, shopping for my upcoming bachelorette party, when the surgeon called me. The good news, he said, was that a lot of people die from things like I'd just been through—I was alive, in other words. But the scar tissue left behind by the blood clots had reduced my lung capacity, and it would take a year or two for the scarring to clear out. That wasn't enough time—the Rio Olympics were a year away. I broke down crying right there in the chips aisle of a Publix supermarket.

✶✶✶

Todd and I got married in East Lansing on August 15, 2015. My bridal party was a "Who's Who" of outstanding women swimmers. My maid of honor was University of South Carolina standout Bridget Halligan, my former T2 teammate. Bridget is the most patient, kind, and selfless person I've ever met—a calming voice whenever I was freaking out about life. Once, at a low point in my life, she stayed on the phone with me while I cried and ate an entire pint of Ben & Jerry's ice cream. My bridesmaids were Erika Erndl (who made the U.S. team for the 2011 Pan Am Games at age 33), Elizabeth Beisel (a three-time Olympian and Olympic medalist), Allison Schmitt (an eight-time Olympic medalist, including three golds), and Caroline Burckle (an Olympic medalist). They would have made an awesome relay team if it weren't for the dresses. One other bridesmaid was Tressa Grummer, my good friend and former roommate from when I was in California. Tressa and I were students at Chapman University together, and she gave me a lot of support at a difficult time in my life, as well as a healthy perspective from someone who was not part of the elite swimmer world. She helped me feel normal. Tressa has gone on to achieve a doctorate in psychology and works in sports psychology. She is also a talented artist, and one of her paintings now hangs in our bedroom. I felt very lucky to be surrounded by such a supportive, driven, and a badass group of women! We had a fantastic two-day bachelorette party in Miami before we flew to East Lansing for the wedding.

We got married at The Peoples Church in East Lansing. Todd's input was minimal. "All I care about is the bride, the bar, and the DJ," he said to me. "Everything else is all you." If they gave out MVP awards at weddings, Todd's mother, Colleen, would have won this one. She helped with the food tasting, arranged the limos, coordinated the reception, and flawlessly took care of many, many other things. Colleen picked The Peoples Church because it had an extra-long center aisle for

me to walk down. The long aisle was important to me. I had planned to take my time getting to the altar, though during the ceremony I practically sprinted. My dad tried to slow me down, but eventually he gave up.

My brother Christian is a professional singer. He sings with the U.S. Army Chorus and is gearing toward a career in musical theater after he's discharged. At the church he sang the Brad Paisley song "Then," and for our first dance, at the reception, he sang "I'll Be," by Edwin McCain. He was wonderful. Both songs were beautiful.

We had the reception at a banquet hall at Spartan Stadium at Michigan State. It went until about 11 p.m., and then we relocated to Harper's, a local bar, and stayed there until around two in the morning. With all the athletes—a lot of Todd's football friends were there—at times it got a little wild. At one point, I remember Beisel grabbing the mic and rapping to a Busta Rhymes' song that typically comes with one of those "Explicit Lyrics" labels.

The only thing throughout the entire day that remotely qualified as a problem was that the air conditioning broke on the van that took us from the church to the reception hall. Everything else was perfect. As I've mentioned, big events have the potential to make me nervous, but at the wedding I felt zero nerves because I had zero reason to be nervous. I was going to walk down the aisle and be married to Todd, and it was going to be amazing. I'd had a number of bad things happen in my life, but my wedding day was an unqualified good thing.

★★★

We went to Cancun for our honeymoon, and on day two thoughts of my grocery store conversation with the doctor about the scar tissue in my lungs came roaring back. Todd was asleep, and I had a meltdown. The doctor had told me, "Okay, you're not going to die, but you're also not going to be able to swim at an elite level anymore. You're not going to be able to do what you've been doing for the past 20 years of your life. You're not going to be able to do the thing that you have been best in the world at doing." I sometimes wonder how the doctor would have taken that news, if someone had told him that he could stay alive, but he wouldn't be able to practice medicine anymore. How would he have responded? So, as I said, there in Cancun, on my honeymoon, I had a meltdown. I felt lost, and I didn't know what to do.

They say the first stage of grief is denial, so that's what I tried to do—deny that my career was over. After we got back to Miami I decided to push forward, altering my training to see if maybe I could compensate for the problems I was experiencing. I went through a couple of months of that, and it went miserably. I talked things over with Todd, with friends, Andy, and my parents. The whole point of a comeback was to enjoy the process, but I wasn't enjoying the process at all. One day in December I went in to see Andy. I said, "This isn't working. I'm going to retire."

After I thanked him for all he'd done and walked back out of his office, I just felt relief. I didn't want to keep crying every day. I didn't want to keep banging my head against the wall. I had become depressed, and I didn't want to be depressed anymore. Ending things this way felt sad, but it also felt right. It was December 2015, I was 26 years old, and I had just retired from swimming.

✶✶✶

In the 1980s a researcher named Bob Goldman asked elite athletes if they would take a drug that would guarantee them an Olympic gold medal, but that would also kill them within five years, would they? About half of the athletes he surveyed said yes. Goldman repeated the survey several times in subsequent years, and the results were always about the same—about half of the athletes surveyed would take a drug that guaranteed gold, but also guaranteed an early death. The question became known as the Goldman dilemma.

It's a question I was never asked to answer, and I'm glad for that. But what if I replace that Faustian bargain with something more along the lines of a Sophie's Choice? I noted a number of pages back that if it hadn't been for my health problems—especially the stomach bug that ruined my Olympic Trials in 2012—there's a good chance that my relationship to Todd might never have unfolded as it did, and it's very possible that I wouldn't have wound up married to him. *So, would I be willing to make a different sort of trade? Would I be willing to sacrifice my relationship to Todd if it meant winning an Olympic gold medal in 2012?*

The short answer is no. The longer answer is that I would be willing to rearrange my past only if it allowed me to have my cake and eat it too. I would let things play out pretty much as they did in 2012. And then I'd meet Todd, and then I'd recover, and then I'd return to the world stage.

In 2016, at the Rio Olympic Games, the U.S. women won gold in the 4 x 200-freestyle relay. If not for the blood clots, there's a really good chance I would have been on that team. So, it's the blood clots I'd get rid of, not my marriage. No way.

TEN FAVORITE
SWIMS

This is where the newly retired swimmer gets to reflect back on her top 10 favorite swims.

1. 2007, World Championships, Melbourne, Australia, the 400-meter individual medley – This one's my number one favorite because it was my first world record.

It was the culmination of three years of work to come back from my disaster of a swim in this same event at the 2004 Olympics in Athens. I raced strategically sound, I felt relaxed, everything about it worked. It was the perfect race.

2. 2005, World Championship trials, Indianapolis, Indiana, the 200-meter individual medley – I set my first American record, and in one of my first big races after the 2004 Olympics. It was very much a vindication swim. The trials were a kind of a breakout meet for me, a way of showing the world that it wasn't a fluke that I'd made the Olympic team in 2004. I remember being so excited and my teammates were all around me. Michael gave me a huge hug. It was my way of saying, "I am here to stay."

3. 2005, World Championships, Montreal, Canada, the 200-meter individual medley – The 200-IM was my first world title, and it came one year after Athens. I got to experience what it was like to stand on the podium and hear the National Anthem. Once again, I felt like I belonged, and now I was competing against the best swimmers in the world.

4. 2004, U.S. Olympic Trials, Long Beach, California, the 400-meter individual medley – I won the race and made my first Olympic team, which made me, at age 15, the youngest American swimmer on the U.S. Olympic Team in 2004. The prelims for this race didn't go quite as well as I'd hoped, but it was a real thrill to rally in the final and make the team. I experienced some odd feelings after trials as the reality of being an Olympian sunk in, sort of like, *Oh, I'm an Olympian—now I have to actually swim at the Olympics?*

5. 2008, U.S. Olympic Trials, Omaha, Nebraska, the 200-meter individual medley and the 200-meter freestyle – I'm cheating a bit here to include two races instead of one, but the 200-IM and the 200-free is a stressful and difficult double, so I'm putting them together here because winning both and setting American records in both on the same night against strong competition made me feel tough and proud. I was on top of the world at that point, having won four races in the first four days of competition.

6. 2007, NBAC Christmas meet, U.S. Naval Academy, Annapolis, Maryland, 1000-yard freestyle – I shattered the American record and sent ripples through the swimming community doing it. I felt so strong and so dominant. I swam a 9:10:77, and even most guys weren't even going that fast. People were asking "What's she on?" meaning drugs (the answer is I wasn't on anything), which I took as a huge compliment.

7. 2010, Short Course World Championships, Dubai, 400-meter freestyle – This one came in the middle of another comeback. It was the first time in a long while that I had an "I got this" feeling in a race. I proved to myself that I still had the strength to win a world title, and it was the first time in two years that I'd felt that.

Watch me regain my
confidence on an
international stage.

8. 1998, Junior Olympics, Newport News, Virginia, 100-meter breaststroke – I was nine years old and broke the state record. In my scrapbook I have a picture of me after the race, and my mouth is wide open in a huge smile. I learned what breaking a record feels like.

9. 2008, U.S. Olympic Trials, Omaha Nebraska, 400-meter individual medley – At the Australian Olympic Trials that year, Stephanie Rice had taken away my world record in the 400-IM. In this race, I took it back. My whole family was there—my mom, my dad, my brother, grandparents, aunts, uncles and cousins. It felt great to share it with my whole family—and it was just this fairytale moment.

10. 2008, Missouri Grand Prix, Columbia, Missouri, 400-meter freestyle – Sometimes you swim a race and something happens that you don't expect. It was an Olympic year, and we were coming off of training camp in Colorado Springs, and in Missouri I broke the American record. This is another one where you can find a picture of me after the race with my mouth wide open. It was so unexpected, and some of the most unexpected races are my favorites.

Missing from this list are games of pool tag, lazy snorkeling expeditions off of tropical beaches, the discovery of a hidden swimming hole in the Rockies (preferably heated by an underground hot spring), things like that. Those aren't what matter to me, and they certainly aren't going to make it onto my list of favorites. I think it's this way for just about all competitive swimmers. It's all about the racing and, with a little luck, the winning.

LUCK

Luck can have different meanings. "Good luck" is a way of wishing someone the best, while saying, "You were lucky" comes across as an insult, an especially painful and unfair one if it ignores all the work, focus, intensity, and relentlessness that may have gone into the "lucky" outcome. Luck can be good or bad. There are times when your luck runs out. But I believe it's a game of ups and downs in life. If you're having a stretch of bad luck, you have to keep pushing so eventually the luck changes from bad to good.

I've had amazing victories and amazingly painful defeats. I think these were less about luck than timing. If you keep pushing and keep trying, and keep your foot on the pedal, eventually it's going to be your time.

NOW WHAT?

The relief I felt at retiring quickly gave way to a question: *Now what?* I'd just dedicated 15 years of my life to being one of the best swimmers in the world. I'd won World Championships, I'd set world records, I'd won Olympic medals. And now, at age 26, I was a former everything—a former World Champion, a former professional athlete. So, now what do I do with my life? And at a more existential level, if I'm not a swimmer, then who am I? I was an unemployed newlywed trying to figure out my next step.

We were still in Miami, and Todd was still working as a fitness manager at Equinox, but he wanted to be closer to family. Through a somewhat convoluted process involving job offers and counteroffers, he was offered a job with Equinox in Chicago, and the offer was a kind of package deal—Equinox had a job for me, too. So we moved to Chicago, and I started out working with Equinox part-time.

Meanwhile, I continued to look for a career that I didn't just stumble into but actively chose. At one point I figured that after I retired from swimming I'd go into fashion. I even had an internship at Bloomingdale's in Miami. But I found it difficult to get too invested in the details of the way a skirt or a blouse in a display window looked, so my career in fashion ended before it ever began.

My next career thought was to become a dietitian. I was interested in food and nutrition, especially as they applied to performance, so it seemed to make sense, even if it posed some obstacles. I'd finished my bachelor's degree at the University of Miami, but it was in public relations, with a minor in sociology. It didn't include courses in subjects like chemistry and biology, courses that I needed to be a dietitian. After we moved to Chicago, I started taking courses in those subjects at a local college while juggling my work with Equinox. I learned that being a dietitian was not for me. I knew in just a few months that I was in the wrong field, and I dropped out of school. Todd was pretty sure he saw where all of this was headed from the outset, but he wisely stood back and let me figure it out on my own.

Meanwhile I was watching the sales teams at Equinox and getting intrigued by what they were doing. *Maybe a salesperson is what I wanted to be.* I called Griff Long, Equinox's vice president of operations, and Eilis Fyda, a regional sales director, both of whom had become mentors for me at Equinox, and I asked them if they had room for another salesperson in Chicago. They said they did. So I began selling gym memberships for Equinox.

When I was nine years old, I didn't hang posters of famous salespeople on my bedroom wall. I didn't read in magazines about sales quotas and marketing strategies and proclaim, "That's what I want to do when I grow up." So here I was in an area that I just sort of fell into.

For the first few months everything was new, and I immersed myself in first learning my job, and then becoming good at it. I liked that, much like swimming, sales were measurable—with performance expectations quotas—monthly sales goals replaced swimming sets and pace times. This played well to my obsessive tendencies. And I'd managed to bury some of the unresolved elements of my past—my Olympic results and relationships with coaches and other matters that would resurface later. I made steady progress, even though sometimes those unresolved elements would rear their ugly head. I had a rough time at Equinox one day in the summer of 2016 when the Rio Olympics were underway and on television; I had to leave my desk and go into the bathroom to cry. I felt like I belonged there in Rio with the other athletes, and I was still devastated that I didn't get an opportunity to actually enjoy the moments of swimming at an Olympic Games. I felt like I had been robbed by my career getting cut too short when I was actually enjoying it for the first time in a long time. It was challenging and so emotional to even hear the Olympic theme song.

But for the most part, I managed to stay focused on my position. It may just have been an entry-level job, but I excelled at it and became one of the Equinox's top sales people in Chicago. I was professionally persistent—transferring some of the energy I used to exert in the pool into selling memberships. I became a hard person to say no to.

About six or seven months into the job, I started to get frustrated. When people I sold to would find out who I was, they would say, "Wait—you're an Olympian, and you're doing this?" It was hard for me to get too excited about a $500 sales bonus, for example, when a year or two before I could make $50,000 for a single swim. There was value in what I was doing—selling Equinox memberships meant selling a healthy lifestyle—but I struggled to feel fulfilled.

It may come as a surprise to a lot of people that professional swimming has real money linked to it, and swimmers can command the kind of profile that would earn them serious money. I knew people who had built on their swimming success and carved out lucrative careers after they stopped swimming. People I competed with were off giving speeches and doing swimming clinics and earning a lot more money that way than I could at Equinox. It wasn't just about the money, or even mainly about the money—it was more about what the money represented, about regaining the kind of professional stature I had become used to. And it wasn't that I didn't have options. It was just that those options meant opening up about my past, and, at the time, my past still felt raw, with too many painful memories there for me to open up about. I had this internal battle with myself—I had become successful at sales, but at the same time I asked myself, *is this really what I want? Am I going anywhere, or am I just treading water?* I felt very ordinary and mediocre.

✶✶✶

Todd is wired a lot like I am. We're both determined. We both can be stubborn. We aren't the most patient people in the world. At this time, we were both young, in our mid-20s, and we both wanted to move up in the world while feeling we were making an impact in some way. In 2017 an opportunity came along that looked like it would enable us to do those things. A new fitness club was starting in the Chicago suburb of Naperville, in a gorgeous facility with all the usual resources plus swim tanks where I could do stroke analysis for clients. We could get in on the ground floor. We're both what you might call "calculated risk-takers," and we felt that if we were going to take a risk, this was the time to do it. We were going to get in with this new company, they were going to make us equity partners; looked great. So we took the gamble and left Equinox.

For reasons I won't go into, it didn't work out. Todd went back to Equinox. I chose not to.

Our friend Griff Long had left Equinox to become chief operating officer of Pure Barre, a fitness franchise that built full body workouts around ballet-based exercises. He offered me a job as a franchise business manager, overseeing Pure Barre franchises throughout the Midwest, and I accepted.

MEDIOCRITY

Mediocrity is my greatest fear. From a very young age I equated mediocrity with just being normal, and normal meant the opposite of extraordinary. One time when I was little, my dad and I were driving down some street in our neighborhood and I saw these two girls walking along aimlessly, doing the most normal thing in the world, and I completely prejudged them. I said, "Look at those girls, they're so ordinary. I never want to be like that."

My dad challenged me. "What do you mean?" he said. "They're just walking."

"They aren't doing anything extraordinary with their lives," I said.

I don't know how this idea got into my head at such a young age, but it got stuck there. Worrying that I'm just mediocre has been a major source of any sadness, frustration, and feelings of inadequacy I've had. Since I've quit swimming, I've felt mediocre many times. If I feel I'm just doing what anyone could do, I get upset and depressed. I feel like I'm losing at life.

This is probably not healthy. It's probably not rational. But it's a feeling I can't shake. And it's the reason I keep striving.

TED

A bright spot, in a career derailed by blood clots, was Xarelto. Xarelto is a blood thinner that my doctor prescribed to reduce my risk of having any recurring blood clots, and it has worked well for me. A number of athletes had taken it, including basketball player Chris Bosh, NASCAR driver Brian Vickers, and golf champion Arnold Palmer, all three of whom had promoted it in commercials. Ever the observant one, my mom pointed out that all three of them were male, and Xarelto might just want to have a female athlete on its promotional team. After months of back and forth with Janssen, the pharmaceutical company that makes Xarelto, I signed on to promote it. I flew to Los Angeles to make a commercial. I went to conventions all over the country and gave speeches with doctors who were specialists in pulmonary embolisms and deep vein thrombosis and other things Xarelto was designed to help with. Janssen paid me well to do all of this.

Meanwhile I also had the job with Pure Barre, though I wasn't loving it. I could appreciate that a lot of people associated with the organization were passionate about their jobs and what Pure Barre did, but I struggled to share those feelings. During that time, I'd kept in touch with Eilis Fyda, from Equinox. I told her how I felt less than fulfilled at Pure Barre, and she talked me into returning to Equinox. My position would be virtually the same one I left, selling gym memberships, but if I was patient, there was a chance that with time (granted, an undefined amount of time) I could move up to be an account executive.

I went back to Equinox, but I struggled with my emotions. I talked to Eilis and Matt Palmer, the general manager, who was another good friend, I told them I couldn't keep it up. But they encouraged me to keep trudging on, so I did. However, the work took a toll on me, and on Todd. I was so stressed out, obsessing over sales quotas while feeling general dissatisfaction with what I was doing with my life. I felt like I was a huge burden on him. I was moody and depressed. My life for as long as I could remember had been about competing to be the best in the world at what I did. I felt no burning passion to be the best in the world at selling gym memberships.

But if not sales, then what? I needed to find something to do that I could do well, something personally and professionally satisfying that wouldn't leave me an emotional wreck at the end of the day.

I liked doing the commercials and appearances for Xarelto. I felt like I was taking this terrible trauma that happened to me and turning it into something positive—a way to help other people. I found that I liked getting up in front of people and telling my story. I had started doing public appearances again—things like Polar Bear plunges or talking to kids in high schools. I liked doing these too. And the more I did, the more comfortable I felt.

In the spring of 2019, the University of Illinois approached me about doing a TEDx talk. At first, I almost blew them off. I was so wrapped up in and stressed out by my work with Equinox, that I felt like I didn't have time for it. But around that time, I had also started thinking that it wouldn't hurt for me to say yes to more things. So I said, "yes" to the TEDx talk.

A TEDx talk follows the same basic format as a regular TED talk. You walk around on stage in a darkened auditorium delivering an impassioned speech about some topic or another to an audience that, if all goes well, sits there listening entranced before standing and applauding enthusiastically at the end. I had seen TED talks, but I had no idea how much work went into them. Some people who do TED talks hire speech coaches to help them prepare, and here I was just doing it on my own.

"This is serious stuff," Todd said to me when I told him about it. "Are you sure you're ready for this?"

I told him not to worry. I wasn't worried. I had done speeches before. I'd done clinics. I didn't figure this would be a whole lot different. I had five weeks to get ready, and that seemed like plenty of time.

I had no idea all that would go into it. I had a series of Skype calls where I would work through the ideas for my speech with the people coordinating the event. I had to create an outline and send it in for review. I had to figure out how I was going to talk for 18 whole minutes, which, I came to understand, is a really long time to be standing up in front of a crowd and talking. And the crowd wasn't going to be swimming people—it would mostly be students and other university staff along with people who lived in the area. So whatever I talked about for 18 minutes would have to resonate with a general audience. I had to memorize my speech—when you give a TED talk you can't have notes or a teleprompter or anything like that—you have to do it from memory.

I practiced and practiced. I began to get nervous. As we got closer to the day of the talk, I felt even more nervous. I practiced one night in the kitchen in front of Todd and my in-laws, mostly just looking at the floor and not at them, just saying the words and not putting a lot of feeling behind them. That just left everyone feeling more worried.

✳✳✳

The theme of my talk was about the value of being relentless, of approaching life with a relentless spirit. "Being relentless," I told the audience at the University of Illinois, "is what drove me through the ups, downs, and challenges of my career."

Watch my talk.

My talk ran about 18 and a half minutes, and the first 17 minutes or so were all about my swimming career. And most of what I said was positive. I talked about wanting to be an Olympian as a young girl, about making the Olympic team in 2004, about surviving the Hell Set Paul assigned to me after the 2004 Games, about the honor of being called the "female Phelps," about winning races and setting records. At one point I even showed a clip from the race in Melbourne where I set my first world record. But I also talked about the bad stuff, about throwing up on the pool deck in Athens in 2004, and about the frustrations I felt as I fell short of achieving "my ultimate goal" of winning an Olympic gold medal. I talked about times when I didn't like my silver and bronze Olympic medals very much, and this was the first time I had confessed this to anyone outside of a very small circle of family and close friends. I talked about my blood clots, how they derailed my career and the devastation I felt. I talked about retiring in 2015, at 26, an age when a lot of people are just starting to see their careers begin to take off.

"For 20 years I was Katie the swimmer," I said, strutting around the TEDx stage in my black pantsuit and heels, trying my best to display more confidence than I was actually feeling. "Now I had to figure out who Katie the person could be."

The subtext of my talk was that this ability to be relentless in the pursuit of something, only really works when you have been able to identify something you care enough about to make that relentless pursuit worth it. Being relentless, in other words, raises a question—relentless in the pursuit of what? Being relentless is only satisfying, for me or for anyone, if you're able to define a goal that completes you. For me, for most of the first 20 years of my life, what completed me was the goal of being the best in the world in swimming.

But the truth was, for people who hadn't found that thing that made relentless pursuit worth it, I really didn't have a lot of great advice. I didn't know how to tell them to find it. And one very good reason for this was that after I had retired from swimming, I hadn't found it either. For most of my life I'd found that thing in the pool, but now, I didn't know what it was or where to look. I made some vague comment about being in "the corporate world," as if the thriving corporate world Katie was who the new Katie would work relentlessly to become. But I knew as I said those words that corporate Katie wasn't the answer, or at least that the corporate world I was then inhabiting wasn't the answer. In order to be relentless, I told the audience, I needed to feel extraordinary at what I was doing. What I didn't tell the audience was that I wasn't feeling particularly extraordinary at the moment.

I realize that all of this could sound like I'm dumping on Equinox. I'm not. Equinox is a great company, and I fully appreciate all the opportunities the people at Equinox have given me. I met a lot of fantastic people there, and to this day

Todd and I are still good friends with them. But for me, trying to feel successful and fulfilled at Equinox was like trying to wear a really nice outfit that didn't quite fit right. It might have looked great on someone else, but it wasn't right for me. And the problem wasn't really with Equinox—I could have been in a similar situation in any number of places in the corporate world and the same feelings of frustration would have surfaced.

I did begin to feel kind of extraordinary in the process of preparing and giving my Tedx Talk. I had to practice my talk. I had to practice how to stand and move. I had to practice which words to emphasize. Before I went on stage, I felt the same adrenaline rush I used to feel before a race. And to the extent that people could connect the ups and downs of their own lives to the highs and lows and painful parts of my swimming career, the talk served a valuable purpose. It made an impact. The whole experience felt kind of cathartic. It made sense. It gave me a feeling of peace. For me, the process of doing the TEDx talk became part of a process of self-discovery. It became a way for me to figure out what could come next—my new purpose.

"It doesn't matter what you're doing," I said at the end of my talk, "as long as you can define that goal that means more to you than anything else, the relentless spirit will rise up." I'd just spent the better part of four years feeling lost, flitting from one thing to another, groping around for that goal. By doing the TEDx talk, had I found it? *Was the feeling I felt the relentless spirit rising up again?*

✷✷✷

Facing the painful parts of my past didn't come easy. I was a wreck watching the Olympics in 2012 when NBC surprised me by showing a clip of a race that I had lost four years earlier. I felt somewhere between ambivalent and shameful about having Olympic medals that were silver and bronze, but not gold. I didn't like how things had gone in my relationship with Paul.

There were so many things that had happened in my career that I wasn't comfortable with. I started going to therapy in Chicago for help. I just didn't want to face my past. I could stand up in front of little kids and give them this unrelentingly positive message, but it wasn't an altogether genuine message. It didn't reflect what I was really feeling deep inside. I was just trying to say what people expected me to say. Until the TEDx talk, I didn't know how to talk about my career in a way that was honest and authentic—a way that could have a positive impact on people.

The Tedx Talk had gone well. It has never attracted a huge audience—a small crowd of 300 saw it in person and about 1300 have watched it online. In contrast, 63,000 have watched the video of Todd's proposal to me at the Tampa Bay Rays game, and, in even greater contrast, millions of people have watched funny cat videos online. But the people who did watch it responded well to it. More importantly, I responded well to it. I liked the process. I discovered that I could be vulnerable and authentic. I learned that the only way I could find real meaning in my swimming career was by going back into all of it and embracing the parts that were painful. Maybe this was a kind of fearlessness, or maybe it was more a matter of finally being able to face what I was afraid of. I'm not sure. But it gave me this confidence.

About a dozen people gave TEDx talks at the University of Illinois the day I gave mine, and one of them was a woman named Dona Sarkar, an executive with Microsoft. She gave a talk on the imposter syndrome, which is where you find yourself in a situation that you don't think you deserve. She took me aside afterward. After you give a talk on a TED stage, everyone says, "Oh, great job—you were wonderful." But what Dona said was different. She gave me constructive feedback. She gave me advice on my delivery and my message. And I could tell by the way she talked to me that she had thought I'd had something meaningful to say. We talked about the work of getting up in front of people and telling my story, and she seemed to envision a future that was only beginning to materialize for me. "You need to do this," she said.

That night when Todd and I were driving home, it was the first time in a long time that I felt proud and excited about what I'd done. I'd begun to see what my future might look like.

✳✳✳

There's an expression that goes, "athletes die twice," meaning once when they actually die, but once, earlier, when they step away from their sport. The average age when professional athletes retire from their sports is 33, and that word—retire— seems strange to apply to someone that young. Some athletes thrive after they retire, going on to satisfying careers in sports or other walks of life, but some don't. Some spiral into lives full of depression, financial problems, drug abuse, and other difficulties. When I retired from swimming at age 26, I wasn't entirely sure which category I would fall into. I wasn't broke or taking drugs, but my struggle with depression was real and difficult.

Some people didn't take my retirement altogether seriously, refusing to believe that professional swimming qualified as a real career. I found this insulting. I felt that what I had experienced as a professional swimmer for the past 10 years grew me up faster than what a lot of people experience in careers three and four times that long. It was hard to make the transition from a career of winning races, setting records, and being well compensated, to how elegantly I had structured an email. That type of transition plays with your head.

When I signed with Speedo in 2005, at age 16, I fully expected that I'd swim in five Olympic Games, through 2020. That was my horizon, and I didn't try to look too hard at what might lie beyond it. I felt that to even begin thinking about what would happen after swimming might not be smart, as it would mean that I was assuming I would encounter some sort of failure that could end my career. It was sort of like why no one wants to tell a baseball pitcher in the seventh inning that he's got a no-hitter going, because they don't want to jinx it. When blood clots did in fact end my career, I had some very unformed ideas about what might come next—fashion, dietetics, public relations—but I didn't have a real plan. So, I ended up taking the dedication and work habits that worked well for me in swimming, and applied them to career steps that never felt quite right for me.

I'm fine with struggle, but the struggle has to be worth something. I invested a lot of time working to become an Olympian because it was worth it to me. But putting in crazy hours and paying my entry-level dues for years so I could rise to the top of...what? A company sales performance ladder? That just wasn't doing it for me. The obsession was still there, but the passion wasn't, and without the passion I felt lost.

✶✶✶

It feels a little strange to follow up with the news that in the spring of 2019, not long after my TEDx talk, Equinox offered Todd and me promotions that would mean we would have to move to New York City. Eilis Fyda would be there, too, and she thought it would be good for us. I like Eilis, and I trusted her. She's very loyal, and I admired how much she fought for the people on her team. I had a lot of respect for how she had managed her career, and I also had confidence in her advice for my career. We said, "yes."

✶✶✶

In New York, Todd was promoted to area manager, which meant he would oversee the personal training operations at three Equinox clubs. My new job was corporate account executive, responsible for developing new client partnerships in and around Midtown Manhattan and Wall Street.

It didn't take long for me to get frustrated. The bottom line for me was that working hard in the corporate world didn't have the same correlation with results that working hard in the swimming world had. As an account executive, I could set up the most events and bring in the most leads and still not hit my budget for the month, and that was infuriating for me. It was hard to find that extraordinary feeling when I didn't feel like I could really make an impact. That was true at Equinox, and it probably would have been true if I had walked down the street to another company. I wasn't happy. In November 2019, I resigned from Equinox.

WHO I AM

I am outgoing, competitive, and strong. I'm vain. I'm authentic. I can be insecure. I'm obsessive and competitive. I need a purpose to do anything. Whatever I do has to be something extraordinary in order for me to feel happy, and I need to be overprepared in order to do that thing in an extraordinary way. I am acutely sensitive to what others think, or to what I think others think, but I'm working on it. I'm optimistic. I'm a worrier. I'm vulnerable, sometimes to a fault. I'm okay at empathy, but I can be inconsistent with it. Sometimes I'm selfish. I'm impatient, which can be both a strength and a weakness. I'm full of contradictions, but then, who isn't?

EMBRACING
THE SUCK

Let's go back for a minute. It's 2004, early on an autumn Friday morning, about three and a half weeks after the Olympic Games in Athens. I've arrived for practice at the North Baltimore Aquatic Center's Meadowbrook pool, where my coach has just told me that today will be the day where I have to swim the dreaded Hell Set. Over the next two and a half hours, I will swim 10,000 yards, nearly six miles, and because my specialty is the individual medley, I will swim part of it butterfly, part of it backstroke, part of it breaststroke, and part of it freestyle. And then when I finish that, when I'm good and exhausted, just for laughs I'll swim another 800 yards of those same strokes as if it were a timed race.

Why am I doing all of this? Because at age 15, I had underachieved in Athens, and the Hell Set figured to help make me better prepared for the challenges that would come my way next in my swimming career. Better prepared for success, in other words, and it makes total sense to me that the first syllable of success is pronounced suck, and if I wanted to get to where I wanted to go, I figured I might as well embrace it.

To get to success, in other words, you have to embrace the suck. "Embrace the suck" is a military expression—warrior slang—that basically means the situation is tough, but you're just going to have to deal with it. Embracing the suck of a Hell Set, or of any other particular workout or meet or championship, or of any kind of big challenge in any walk of life, also means embracing the possibility of failure along the way. Failure is just part of the process, and it comes with its share of pain, tears, and moments of despair. Once you accept this, and embrace it, the suck may not go away, but it begins to lose its power over you. Embracing the suck is a big part of who I am. It's why I've been able to pick myself up after some pretty major setbacks and keep going.

I am inspired by people like Sir James Dyson. *Who is Sir James Dyson?* Sir James Dyson is a British inventor and industrial designer best known for inventing the Dual Cyclone bagless vacuum cleaner, a field of endeavor that's about as far away from swimming as you can get. What inspires me about Mr. Dyson is not that he invented a vacuum cleaner, but that it took him 15 years and 5,126 prototypes before he developed the vacuum cleaner that would make him one of the richest people in Britain and a legend in the world of industrial design. "There were 5,126 failures, but I learned from each one," he told *Fast Company* in 2007, in an article that I promise you is titled "Failure Doesn't Suck." I find it doubly interesting that when he was young, Mr. Dyson excelled at long-distance running, which he said he was good at "not because I was physically good, but because I had more determination."

Four years after the Hell Set, in 2008, I was at the top of my game. I had won World Championships. I had set world records. I had been compared to Michael Phelps. I had gone through a couple of earlier Katie Hoff prototypes and wound up with one that was working out really well for me. And then came the Beijing Olympics. I went to Beijing with super high expectations—expectations I placed on myself and expectations placed on me by others inside and outside the world of swimming. But even though I swam pretty well, I came home without living up to those expectations. Beijing turned out to be my last best shot at Olympic gold, as in the years that followed, health problems brought an abrupt and painful ending to my swimming career. And that's a suck that's been tough to embrace!

How would my life be different if I'd swum eight hundredths of a second faster and won the 400-freestyle in Beijing in the summer of 2008, instead of touching second by less time than it takes to blink an eye? Or how would my life be different if I'd won gold the day before in the 400-individual medley, my strongest event, the one I was favored to win?

Trust me, I've given this plenty of thought.

For one, my relationship with Paul might have worked out differently, and for the better. The other races I swam in Beijing might have worked out better, too, races I swam with a sense of desperation and panic as I felt gold slipping through my fingers. Maybe with some of the pressure to win gold removed, I would have won a medal in one or more of those races. And maybe I would feel more complete.

I will go to my grave frustrated in knowing that I never achieved my goal of becoming an Olympic champion. I wanted it. I worked for it with all my soul, but it eluded me—I'm never going to be able to get it. It's taken years, but I'm finally ready to embrace that too.

What's helped me get to the other side of this is knowing that the pursuit of that unique and extraordinary goal made me feel unique and extraordinary. And the effort that went into that pursuit, the manner in which I approached it, is part of who I am.

BLUEPRINT

David and Goliath. The '69 Mets. Rocky. The Miracle on Ice. The world loves a good story about the overachieving underdog. But what about the underachieving overdog? If you measure my career solely by what happened at two Olympic Games, that's how a lot of people saw me. Michelangelo didn't sculpt a famous statue of Goliath, after all.

I had a precocious swimming career, climbing onto the global stage when I was a naive teenager. I also had a successful swimming career, full of American records and world records and wins—and yes, Olympic medals—in races where I competed against the best swimmers on the planet. I was labeled the female Phelps. But expectations came with that label. Like the male Phelps, I was supposed to wind up my career in possession of a lot of Olympic-branded gold jewelry. But things didn't work out that way. Did I underachieve? In my own mind, no. Did I meet those expectations—expectations that, let's be fair, I didn't exactly discourage? Well, no.

$$\star\star\star$$

My mom sings with a jazz ensemble in Baltimore. Just before Christmas in 2019, I was visiting her and my dad, and I went to hear the group perform at a church. Afterward, we all went to a restaurant nearby for the after party. Someone had told the husband of one of the singers that I had been an Olympic swimmer, and he came over and sat down next to me and wanted to talk. There were two things he wanted to know. One, did I know Michael Phelps? (Yes.) And two, did I ever win an Olympic gold medal? (No, but it's complicated.)

The neat and tidy way to end this book would be with some sort of transcendent message about how a person should live their life. But I have no such message. This is just my story, about a lifelong struggle to find out what makes me feel fulfilled, a struggle that hasn't gotten any easier now that I'm no longer doing that one thing, that for most of my life, I was the best at.

A blueprint is basically a plan, and people have been weighing in on the importance of having a plan and the folly of trying to follow one for centuries. We have heard from poets ("The best laid [plans] o' mice an' men...;" Robert Burns), authors ("A goal without a plan is just a wish;" Antoine de St. Exupéry), world leaders ("...plans are useless, but planning is indispensable;" Dwight D. Eisenhower), philosophers ("If you don't know where you're going, you'll wind up someplace else;" Yogi Berra), and many, many others.

When I was a little girl I had an image in my mind of what being an Olympian meant, a glorified image that failed to take into account the amount of work that would go into becoming an Olympic athlete or the amount of pressure I would be under once I became one. My plan was simple—an Olympic athlete was what I wanted to be, and my blueprint for how to get there went no further than the posters of swimmers I idolized that were thumbtacked to my bedroom walls. I just wanted to be like them.

When I made my first Olympic team, I had no idea how my dreams of becoming an Olympian would turn into nightmares, like when I puked all over the Athens pool deck. Four years later I was the odds-on favorite to win multiple gold medals at the Olympics in Beijing, and when that didn't happen, I had to pivot, revise, and figure out what would come next. When I signed a professional contract with Speedo at age 15, I expected to be swimming professionally in London in 2012, Rio in 2016, and all the way through the Tokyo Olympics in 2020 (pre-Covid19). Health problems shattered that dream, and since then I've had to figure out who I am now that I'm no longer Katie the swimmer.

Doing something I'm passionate about. Feeling extraordinary. Feeling like my life could inspire others. Those are the buttons that being a swimming champion pushed for me. What pushes those buttons now? I keep working on the blueprint, and it's very much a work in progress. If the past is any indication, in whatever I pursue, I'm likely to get knocked on my butt from time to time. But no matter how many times that happens, I plan to keep getting up.

Final parting thoughts.

ABOUT THE AUTHOR

Katie Hoff is a two-time Team USA Olympian, current American record holder and former world record holder.

Katie started swimming at the age of five. Although she "retired" a mere year later, she eventually found her way back to loving the water again, and began training at WAC in Williamsburg, VA.

Her competitive spirit was ignited at a young age, and Katie recalls constantly pushing her brother, friends, and teammates to compete at everything and anything they did. She was so competitive that at just 10 years old, Katie declared she was going to make an Olympic Team. Four-and-a-half years later, Katie was representing Team USA at the 2004 Olympics in Athens.

A year later at World Championships, she won three gold medals, and broke her first American record in the 200-individual medley. Two years after that, Katie broke her first world record in the 400-individual medley. And then at the 2008 Beijing Olympics, Katie was on the podium in three events, walking away with two bronze and one silver medal. In 2012, Katie missed qualifying for the U.S. Olympic Team due to illness. This persuaded her to move to Miami Beach and finish school at the University of Miami.

Katie officially retired from the sport of swimming in 2015 after being diagnosed with a pulmonary embolism. She took her competitive spirit to the corporate world, joined the sales team at Equinox, and was quickly named one of their top sales representatives. Katie was then promoted to Corporate Account Executive, which provided her the opportunity to work closely with many Fortune 500 companies to incorporate wellness into the workplace.

Katie and her husband Todd recently moved from New York City to Royal Oak, Michigan, to be closer to family and to pursue different career opportunities. They launched their own dryland company, Synergy Dryland, meant to empower swimmers and teams to develop strength that correlates to swimming fast in the pool.

Katie continues to share her story of resilience, finding an extraordinary life, and embracing the suck.

Check out Synergy Dryland.

USA Olympic And Career Highlights

- 2x USA Olympian: 2004 & 2008
- 3x Olympic Medalist
- 8x World Champion
- 18x International Medalist
- Current American Record Holder, 400m IM
- Former World Record Holder
- 2x USOC Sportswoman of the Year
- TEDx Talk Speaker – "Finding Your Relentless Spirit"
- Board of Governors of the Association of Churchill Fellows Guest Speaker
- AMWA Centennial Meeting Guest Speaker
- Keynote speaker at Jesse Itzler's Build Your Life Resume Camp

   Keynote Speaking Topics:
   - Embracing the suck to your extraordinary
   - Process makes perfect
   - How to be relentless

Made in the USA
Middletown, DE
03 December 2020